THE DEADLIEST

FIRES THEN AND NOW

A photo from September 2020 depicts another severe fire season in California, with dozens of fires, some of them deadly.

THE DEADLIEST

FIRES THEN AND NOW

BY

**DEBORAH
HOPKINSON**

SCHOLASTIC
F🜨CUS

NEW YORK

Library of Congress Cataloging-in-Publication Data available

ISBN   978-1-338-36025-7

1 2022

Printed in the U.S.A.   23
First edition, May 2022

Book design by Abby Dening

Photograph, previous page: Firefighters worked to control
hundreds of wildfires in California in 2020. Scientists point to
global climate change as one factor in the increase of severe
wildfires throughout the American West and in other parts of the
world.

For Meghan, Drew, and Arden

Contents

PROLOGUE
A Tiny Tongue of Fire

Father Peter Pernin longed for rain, but no rain came. Week after week in the summer of 1871, he scanned the sky, hoping for an end to the drought and relief for the dry, parched earth.

As that dry summer slid into fall, Father Pernin became more worried than ever. Small fires seemed to stalk the forests around Peshtigo (pronounced PESH-tih-go). Father Pernin was born in France. Now he served as a Roman Catholic priest in this booming Wisconsin lumber town of about two thousand people on the western shore of Green Bay.

Fire seemed to be everywhere. Flames whispered in the branches of magnificent pines and lurked underfoot in the crisp, withering leaves of oak, maple, beech, and elm. Debris left by loggers clogged the forest floor, making the woods more vulnerable to large fires. Railway workers cut trees and left them piled carelessly near the tracks, where sparks from trains could easily ignite piles of logs and brush. And when fires were started to clear brush for new tracks, workers often just left them to burn, and didn't watch or tend them carefully.

Usually, autumn rains doused small fires before they spread. But during that dry fall, Father Pernin could see the forests "gleaming everywhere with fires." And sixteen days before the great tragedy, he came face-to-face with fire.

On Friday, September 22, 1871, after visiting with a family in the Sugar Bush farming community outside town, Father Pernin asked the farmer's twelve-year-old son to be his guide for some pheasant hunting in the woods. As the sun sank, the priest and the boy started back. That's when they ran into trouble.

"We went on and on, now turning to the right, now to the left, but without coming in view of our destination," said Father Pernin. "In less than a half hour's wanderings we perceived that we were completely lost in the woods."

Father Pernin stopped to listen, hoping the boy's family would send out a search party. Instead, he heard "the crackling of a tiny tongue of fire that ran along the ground, in and out, among the trunks of the trees, leaving them unscathed but devouring the dry leaves that came in its way."

Father Pernin shot off his gun to attract attention; he and the boy shouted for help. At last, they heard voices and set off in that direction. But the crackling tongues of fire were spreading fast. And suddenly the pair was surrounded by a circle of fire—a circle closing fast around them. They spotted their friends, but couldn't get to them. They were trapped.

Just in time, the rescuers sprang into action. They grabbed branches and managed to beat back the flames to make a pathway. Father Pernin and the boy sprinted through the smoke as fast as they could, hoping their shoes wouldn't get too scorched.

Father Pernin and his young companion were lucky—this time. But what if wind had fanned the flames into a larger fire? What if the fire had grown and a strong wind had pushed it into town?

For a substance to ignite, or catch fire, the three elements of the **fire triangle** must be present: heat, fuel, and an oxidizing agent such as oxygen. Air contains oxygen and strong winds increase the amount of oxygen in the fire triangle. This speeds up the rate of **combustion.** Combustion is a chemical reaction that produces heat and light. Its most common form is fire. When wood burns, oxygen in the air joins with the carbon in wood.

The addition of air (which is 20 percent oxygen) explains why a campfire burns hotter when we blow on it. And that's why wind in a dry, burning forest can make fires much fiercer. Putting out fires involves removing one or more of these three elements of the fire triangle. That's what happens, for example, when planes drop loads of water on wildland fires or we smother the remains of a campfire with dirt or water.

And it was hard to look at Peshtigo and not see danger everywhere. The houses were wood, along with Father Pernin's new church, the gristmill, and the sawmill. Leftover sawdust from cut logs was stuffed in mattresses, shoveled under the boards of the sidewalks, and piled into great mounds. There was a large woodenware factory too, where two hundred workers made pails, broom handles, shingles, barrel covers, and clothespins—all from wood.

In that fiery autumn, Peshtigo was like a giant box of fuel, just ready to be lit.

BEFORE YOU GO ON

You're about to read about some of the deadliest fires in United States history, beginning with the deadliest of all in Peshtigo, Wisconsin, on October 8, 1871.

Peshtigo is often called "the forgotten fire." It's always been overshadowed by the Great Chicago Fire, which broke out on that same Sunday night. As we'll explore in Part One, this wasn't entirely a coincidence. Although the Chicago disaster is the one people remember, the fires in Peshtigo and Chicago are both part of a larger story—the **Great Midwest Fires of 1871**.

In Part Two, we'll move on to deadly fires of the twentieth century, beginning with the Iroquois Theater in Chicago in 1900. We'll explore how that tragedy, along with others, led to regulations to better protect people in public buildings and cities. We'll see how fire disasters have affected immigrants, workers, and communities of color more severely.

We'll end Part Two by looking back at the deadly wildfire summer of 1910, which will lead us into Part Three. In this section, we'll explore how decades of United States governmental fire suppression policies (putting out *all* fires), along with population growth and global climate change, are leading to more severe wildfires in the twenty-first century. We'll touch on some of the ways U.S. government agency policies to control fires have affected Native Americans in negative ways, and how people are trying to change that.

The challenges we face with wildfires now and in the future are enormous. That's why people are working together to find solutions and create partnerships among scientists, fire experts, Native Americans and other Indigenous peoples, farmers, forest managers, and local communities. People are trying to be open to new ideas and traditional practices, especially those of Native Americans and other Indigenous peoples in the world.

In this book, we use Indigenous to refer to people who are the original inhabitants of a particular place and space. Native American is the term used for Indigenous people from North America, usually the United States.

It takes a lot of people working together to make a book too. I've been guided by the advice of a Native American colleague, who read the manuscript in draft form. A wildfire expert also read the draft and made suggestions to improve information about wildland firefighting. U.S. Forest Service supervisor Merv George, Jr., a member of the Hoopa Valley Tribe, took time from his busy schedule to explain how essential fire has been to Native American communities over many centuries. I appreciate everyone's help, and any mistakes are mine.

Our new world of fire is here—right on our doorsteps—in a rapidly warming climate and more severe weather events. Yet this challenge also brings a chance—and an urgent need—for change. I hope you'll want to be part of it.

On this journey into fires then and now, we'll have several guides: resourceful kids, brave survivors, a famous actor of his time, and intrepid reporters.

Interested in being a journalist or a wildland fire-fighter? We've included interviews by students in the back. There's a section about studying forestry too.

Maybe you've faced deadly fires yourself or know people who have. Whether you have personal experience or not, fire is a complex topic, and this book is only a start. Throughout the book, and in the bibliography and resources in the back, you'll find suggestions for continuing your learning journey and discovering other perspectives.

You've already met our first eyewitness to fires of the past: Father Peter Pernin. He probably never imagined people would be reading his words more than 150 years later.

Father Pernin's harrowing account, one of the most complete we have from Peshtigo, reminds us that we're all part of history. Telling your story is important. Who knows? Someone might read your words hundreds of years in the future.

So let's head back to Peshtigo and catch up with Father Pernin in the days before the deadliest fire in America—then or now.

In this painting, Wisconsin artist Mel Kishner (1915–1991) imagines the deadly fire in Peshtigo, Wisconsin, on October 8, 1871.

Part One

THE NINETEENTH CENTURY
The Great Midwest Fires of 1871

CHAPTER ONE

Peshtigo 1871: A Growing Sense of Dread

A bird's-eye view of Peshtigo with surrounding forests and farms. The Peshtigo River and a bridge separated the village into two.

Father Peter Pernin's close call in the woods in September made him more anxious than ever. You just had to look around to see Peshtigo wasn't prepared if one of those small gleaming fires in the woods got out of control.

To add to his worries, Peshtigo didn't yet have a regular fire department or trained firefighters. The town owed its success in large part to William Butler Ogden, a former mayor of Chicago. Ogden had invested heavily in acres of forestland, the large woodenware factory, a dry goods store, and a boardinghouse. His Peshtigo Company established barge and railroad lines to bring lumber from the forest to sawmills in Peshtigo and then on to Chicago.

The town also boasted a butcher shop, a barber, groceries, a gristmill, two churches, and a new jewelry store. But there was still no firehouse—just one piece of fire equipment operated by a hand pump. It was kept on the east side of the river that divided the town. Father Pernin lived near his church on the west side, just five or six minutes' walk to the river.

Peshtigo residents were primarily White, many of them immigrants or descendants of families who'd come to Wisconsin from Germany, Belgium, France, and other parts of Europe. Before that, French and Canadian fur traders had visited the region. But none were the first people to live here. For these forests were—and still are—the home of the Menominee Indian Tribe of Wisconsin, who have lived with fire and nature from time immemorial. Today the tribe also manages its own forest in a sustainable manner to maintain a healthy forest and provide resources to tribal members. (To learn more about the Menominee Indian Tribe of Wisconsin, see the special section at the end of this chapter.)

While the White residents in Peshtigo may have set fires, intentionally or not, they were not using fire to sustain healthy forests as Indigenous Americans have been doing for thousands of years. Merv George, Jr., U.S. Forest Service forest supervisor of the Rogue River-Siskiyou National Forest in Oregon and California and former tribal council chairman of the Hoopa Valley Tribe of California, spends a lot of time educating people about fire management. And, despite his very busy job, he generously responded to my email asking if he would help us better understand active forest management.

He begins by outlining the difference between "good fires" and "bad fires."

"Good fires are ones that are intentionally lit in areas that have been prepped and in the cooler months of the year," Merv notes. "These **controlled burns** result in low, intense understory burns that clean our forest floors and remove forest litter.

"Tribes and Indigenous people have been practicing this method of active forest management since the beginning of time," he continues. "No lands would have been neglected or left unattended since the forests were the grocery store (home of food sources like deer, elk, huckleberries, acorns, etc.), travel corridors, pharmacy, church, and water supply, to name a few roles the forest plays compared to modern society."

(As we'll explore more in Part Three, tribes in North America and Indigenous people in other parts of the world are fighting to revitalize and reinvigorate these practices, sometimes called cultural burning.)

But in the 1800s, as the nation pushed ever westward, White businessmen, government leaders, and settlers did not think about caring for the landscape and creating healthy forests in this way. And the industrial revolution of the nineteenth century led to an explosion of factories and growth.

The main focus was profits, clearing land for farms and factories, and jobs for a growing population of immigrants. Native Americans continued to be forced off their lands. Forests were a resource to be taken and used.

And so the fires that sprang up around Peshtigo's new railroad weren't being carefully or thoughtfully managed. They weren't being tended as "good" fires. Nor was anyone paying much attention to the piles of brush near the tracks or to the **slash**, debris such as small tree limbs and branches left by loggers in the forests, making the landscape vulnerable to severe "bad" fires.

And this lack of understanding and carelessness led to tragedy.

"Labyrinth of Smoke and Fire"

As more fires flared, Peshtigo residents took some steps to protect their houses and shops, such as cutting down trees close to town. When the sawdust near the woodenware factory broke out in flames, the alarm brought volunteers racing. They formed a bucket brigade, dowsing the fire with pail after pail of water from the Peshtigo River.

There was one small fire, then another, and another. How long could this go on before one of these fires—rolling in from a farm, the railroad line, or the forest—became too large to put out?

In early October, Father Pernin was returning home from Marinette, a town a few miles away. He'd recently built a new church there too. On the road, he encountered a dense cloud of smoke from fires in the woods. He had no choice but to try to go through. "My horse held back, but I finally succeeded in urging him on, and in five or six minutes we emerged safely from this labyrinth of smoke and fire."

A few days of heavy, solid rain would have helped. But no rain came.

Sunday, October 8

Father Pernin wasn't even supposed to be in Peshtigo that day. He'd been invited to say Mass (the Roman

Catholic religious service) in Cedar River, a town to the north. He'd tried to go there on Saturday, waiting on the Peshtigo wharf for the regular steamboat to arrive. It never showed up. Thick smoke along the shore made it too dangerous for the boat to dock.

So Father Pernin had gone home. He held church services in Peshtigo on Sunday morning. After that, he spent a restless day. He just didn't like the look of things. The air was smoky, the sky ominous. Fire seemed to be waiting in the shadows, like a menacing wild beast.

By evening, Father Pernin wondered if he was overreacting. Other people didn't seem that concerned. The boardinghouse and nearby tavern were bustling, full of salespeople, visitors, and railroad workers enjoying themselves. Father Pernin guessed there were at least two hundred young men who'd just arrived in Peshtigo as temporary laborers. They wanted to have some fun, not worry.

Still, Father Pernin couldn't shake his sense of foreboding. At about seven o'clock on Sunday evening, he decided to check in with a neighbor. She too was concerned by the smoky air and sky. They stood in a field by her house. The wind had been blowing from the west all day, and now it came in quick, sharp gusts. It was definitely getting stronger.

As Father Pernin started back toward his house, he looked up. Above the dense cloud of smoke that seemed to hang over the world, he spied a patch of vivid red in the distance. But what startled him most was what he heard.

It was a strange, unearthly sound. And this time, it wasn't the soft crackling of dry leaves like he'd heard in the woods. No. This time Father Pernin heard a muffled but ominous "distant roaring like a rumbling train or deep, heavy thunder." Monstrous and huge, this unseen menace seemed to be racing straight toward town.

In an instant, Father Pernin made up his mind. He would save what he could, then run to the river, where he'd be safe from any wildfire that might strike the town.

At least, he hoped so.

THE MENOMINEE TRIBE OF WISCONSIN

While Peshtigo and other towns were made up mainly of White European immigrants, this region of Wisconsin has long been the home of the Menominee Indian Tribe of Wisconsin, which today holds 276,000 forested acres near Keshena, Wisconsin, about fifty-four miles west of Peshtigo. The Menominee Tribe's ancestral lands once encompassed more than ten million acres.

In modern times, the Menominee Tribe has actively managed some parts of these lands now called the Menominee Forest. The Menominee Tribe's practices of sustainable forestry are a model for the twenty-first century. **Sustainable forestry** management enables tribal members to experience "a traditional quality of life from an intact, diverse, productive, and healthy forest ecosystem on the reservation."

Some of the practices used in managing the Menominee Forest include careful attention to which trees should be harvested, protection of trees from damaging insects and weeds, and, of course, fire management. This can include burning to reduce fuel that might lead to large, damaging fires. Expert foresters grow, harvest, and sell many kinds of lumber, including red oak, white pine, and ash, as well as varieties of maple and birch. Who knows? Maybe you've even walked across a floor that was once a tree in the Menominee Forest.

Visitors to the Menominee Tribe's website can learn more about its history at https://www .menominee-nsn.gov/.

Menominee Tribe Honored

Studying history means confronting difficult truths. Prejudice and racism are part of our past and present. In addition to enslaving African Americans, the United States forced Indigenous Americans from their homelands. And the historical record tells us that Native Americans faced racial hostility and animosity from Whites. Abram Place, a White settler originally from Vermont, may have been an exception. He and his wife, a Native American woman whose English name was Elizabeth, owned a large farm in the Sugar Bush area outside Peshtigo.

We don't know much about them, but in 1871, Abram appears to have valued advice from Elizabeth's family about the threat of fire. It's likely the couple used controlled burning to help reduce the risk of severe fires on their land. It's reported that Menominee relatives and friends helped the Places keep their farmhouse roof wet so stray sparks wouldn't ignite it, and plowed around the house to form a firebreak.

Thanks to that, and possibly some luck, the Place farmhouse was one of few that survived in the Sugar Bush community. Afterward, the family opened their doors as a field hospital to all their neighbors in need.

It took many years, but in 2018, the Menominee Tribe of Wisconsin was given a long overdue award by the Wisconsin State Legislature to honor its service to the community during the Peshtigo fire so long ago.

The recognition took place in November, during National Native American Heritage Month. Perhaps you and your loved ones already participate in National Native American Heritage Month. To find out more about celebrations during National Native American Heritage Month in your area, visit https://nativeamericanheritagemonth.gov/.

CHAPTER TWO
To the River!

Residents rushed to the Peshtigo River to escape the raging fire.

As the terrifying roar drew closer, Father Pernin's first thought was for his horse. The priest turned the animal loose from the stable, hoping it could outrun the flames. Sadly, Father Pernin wasn't able to save his horse, dog, or pet bird. The fire killed many farm animals, as well as birds and wild creatures.

Father Pernin next tried to protect some of the church's religious objects and books by burying them in trunks in his garden. He hoped if the trench was deep enough, the objects might survive. He dug furiously. The wind was blowing even harder now; the sky had turned a strange, ominous red. Most worrying of all was the fearsome sound.

When he finished, Father Pernin threw down his shovel and ran to the church to fetch the sacred chalice used for celebrating Mass. It was kept inside a white wooden box called a tabernacle. He placed the bulky tabernacle in his wagon, thinking it might be easier to pull it than run with it in his arms. Then he set out for the river.

He was almost too late.

"Great Sheets of Fire"

By now, Father Pernin was running through a horrific whirlwind. Giant tongues of flame leaped above the treetops. "The air was no longer fit to breathe, full as it was of sand, dust, ashes, cinder, sparks, smoke, and fire," he said.

"The neighing of horses, falling of chimneys, crashing of uprooted trees, roaring and whistling of the wind, crackling of fire as it ran with lightning-like rapidity from house to house—all sounds were there save that of the human voice. People seemed stricken dumb by terror."

It would have been useless to even try to speak. The fire's voice was all there was. In this horrific chaos, Father Pernin made himself go on. He tripped, and then struggled to his feet. The wind hurled him down once more. He got up again and kept on, driven by his will to survive. He could have gone faster without worrying about the tabernacle, but he was determined to at least *try* to save it. Houses near the river were already bursting into flames. The wind dashed cinders and flames all around him, stinging his face and eyes.

"The roar increased, and burning coals began to

drop in the village, first like stray meteors of the night, and then as thickly as the snows of winter," wrote Frank Tilton, editor of the *Green Bay Advocate*, who interviewed Peshtigo survivors.

"Within a half an hour, and some say within ten minutes of the time the first building caught fire, the entire village was in flames," Frank wrote. "The great sheets of fire curled and rolled over the ground like breakers on a reef. Overhead the air seemed to be on fire. The smoke was so dense that it was next to impossible to see which way to go. . . . At one moment the whole earth would be lighted up with almost the brightness of day, and at the next the darkness would be almost total."

The scene at the river was sheer chaos, with people spilling in from both sides of the village. Some had clustered on the bridge, but it soon caught fire too. Father Pernin found a spot and waded in, pushing the wagon wheels into the water as far as he dared.

He wanted to stay close to the wagon to protect the tabernacle from water and flames. But he soon had to leave it for deeper water—and try to save his own life.

CHAPTER THREE
The Air Was on Fire

The Peshtigo River was a scene of chaos.

Father Pernin had plunged into the river just in time. But as he peered back into the whirlwind of smoke, dust, and cinders, he was horrified to see people still on the riverbank.

His neighbors had gotten this far but now seemed too terrified to move an inch farther. Father Pernin knew standing *beside* the river wasn't going to keep them safe. So he waded back out and dragged one dazed man in. Seeing this, others soon followed, one by one.

By this time, Father Pernin guessed it was about ten o'clock at night. At first, he hoped staying submerged in deep water up to his neck would keep him safe. He was wrong. Anything—hair, hats, shirts, or coats—sticking up above the surface of the water instantly caught fire from flying embers, sparks, and debris.

Some people had grabbed clothing and quilts as they fled, hoping to save a few household items. At first, Father Pernin thought these coverings might help protect people's eyes and heads from the smoke. These too dried quickly and began to burn.

"The flames darted over the river as they did over land, the air was full of them, or rather the air itself was on fire. Our heads were in continual danger. It was only by throwing water constantly over them and our faces, and beating the river with our hands that we kept the flames at bay," Father Pernin said.

The high winds and dry weather on October 8, 1871, also led to deadly wildfires in Michigan towns. This illustration shows refugees in White Rock, Michigan, who, like people in Peshtigo, tried to find safety in the water.

People bobbed, and beat the water with their hands to stay afloat. Everything on shore was now in flames. The woodenware factory had a store attached, with tubs, buckets, and other items for sale. It burned in less than fifteen minutes.

The fire made the river as bright as day. In the eerie light, Father Pernin saw a cow swim past. It rammed into a log to which a woman was clinging. Her head sank under the water. Father Pernin thought she was lost. But she emerged, clinging desperately to the cow's horns. He found out later that both survived.

Terrible minutes passed. Then one hour, then two, and three. People began to tremble and shake with cold. Father Pernin kept moving, throwing water over his head and over people next to him. At one point, he started to walk up on the riverbank to get warmer. Someone shouted, "'Father, beware, you are on fire!'" And so he turned back.

Almost Lifeless

It's hard to imagine that nightmarish ordeal. But little by little, the fire became less ferocious. At about three thirty in the morning, after nearly six hours in the water, Father Pernin thought the fire had died down enough that it would be safe to get out.

He dragged himself from the river and sat on a log on the bank. He was trembling violently; someone threw a blanket over him. Like everyone else, he was in shock.

The survivors faced a new danger. They'd been submerged for hours in a chilly river. Now they were exposed to the night air, and their bodies were growing even colder by the minute. Father Pernin moved near some smoldering fragments. That helped dry his outer garments, but he still couldn't stop shivering.

It's likely that Father Pernin and others were suffering from **hypothermia,** which happens when one's body temperature drops dangerously low, usually after exposure to the cold. Hypothermia is a life-threatening condition; today, people are treated in the hospital. Other survivors had suffered burns. But there were no hospitals anywhere nearby, and no help on the way.

Father Pernin felt pressure on his chest; his throat felt raw and swollen. "I could scarcely use my voice— utter even a word," he said. "Almost lifeless, I stretched myself out full length on the sand. The latter was still hot, and the warmth in some degree restored me. Removing shoes and socks I placed my feet in immediate contact with the heated ground, and felt additionally relieved."

The worst pain came from his eyes, which were irritated and inflamed from the smoke, ashes, cinders, and heat. Father Pernin could barely open them.

And then, slowly, it became light.

CHAPTER FOUR
Heartbreak and Horror

The ruins of Peshtigo, Wisconsin.

As darkness faded, the survivors saw the horrors night had hidden. Their town was in ruins; only part of a single building remained. But that was not the worst. The worst was the unimaginable loss of life.

In the frantic effort to escape, many families had become separated. Some fathers had stayed behind, hoping to fight the blaze and save their family's home. Instead, they'd been caught by the fast-moving, ferocious fire. Mothers had tried to run, holding on to little ones, only to have them swept from their arms in the fierce firestorm. Many of the young workers about to start their new jobs on the railroad hadn't left the tavern in time. Would their families ever know how they had died?

It took a long time for survivors to recover and heal. For many, the heartache and trauma would last a lifetime. Even for Father Pernin, who hadn't been burned or lost a family member, recovery wasn't easy. One reason he wrote the story of his ordeal was to sell copies to raise money to rebuild his churches in Peshtigo and in the nearby town of Marinette, which also burned. At the same time, telling his story may have helped him come to terms with the grief of losing so many friends and neighbors.

A Tornado of Fire

Telling his story came later, of course. In the early hours of Monday, October 9, Father Pernin felt barely alive. When a dying woman asked for him, he tried to comfort her. But, he remembered, "I could not unclose my inflamed eyes, could scarcely speak, and felt so exhausted and depressed myself, that it was difficult to impart courage to others."

One man walked several miles to Marinette to fetch help. Meanwhile, survivors from the Sugar Bush farming community outside town straggled into what was left of Peshtigo. Their stories were often more tragic, since people hadn't been able to run to a river close by. The fire had swept through the fields like a tornado, leaving only a few houses standing and killing entire families.

A farmer named Alfred Griffin who managed to survive later told journalist Frank Tilton, "'When I heard the roar of the approaching tornado I ran out of my house and saw a great black, balloon-shaped object whirling through the air over the tops of the distant trees, approaching my house. When it reached the house it seemed to explode, with a loud noise, belching out fire on every side, and in an instant my house was on fire in every part.'"

Those who lived told incredible stories. Some had pressed themselves into ravines or lay flat on the ground, digging small holes to help breathe. Others had tried to hide in wells, root cellars, potato fields, or creek beds.

One mother managed to harness their frightened team of horses to plow a deep furrow in the field, then covered her children with dirt. The family went to the field hospital at the home of Abram and Elizabeth Place to recover.

Survivors emerged at daylight into a strange, blackened landscape, strewn with smoking ruins, burned and fallen trees, and unthinkable sorrow.

Scorched, Cold Cabbage

At first, there was little to eat or drink—all the food in town had gone up in flames. Father Pernin longed for a warm mug of coffee or tea; what he got was something quite different.

"Some of the young men, after a close search, found and brought back a few cabbages from a neighboring field. The outer leaves, which were thoroughly scorched, were removed and the inner part cut into thin slices and distributed among those capable of eating them," the priest said. "A morsel of cold cabbage was not likely to prove of much use in our then state of exhaustion, but we had nothing better at hand."

In the afternoon, the first help arrived from Marinette: wagons with bread, coffee, and tea. Marinette had been hit by fire too, but had fared better. The townspeople had escaped. However, many buildings besides Father Pernin's church had been destroyed.

Friends in Marinette opened their home to the priest, and he recovered there for two nights before returning to Peshtigo on Wednesday. As he walked through the remains of what had been a vibrant, thriving town, it was hard to grasp what had happened.

"Of the houses, trees, fences that I had looked on three days ago nothing whatever remained, save a few blackened posts still standing," Father Pernin said.

Every step landed in ashes. The iron tracks of the railroad were twisted into strange shapes. Huge trees had been reduced to cinders; even the roots had burned away beneath the ground, leaving empty, snaking tunnels. While most of the human victims had been buried, there hadn't yet been time to dispose of the charred bodies of livestock.

Like a Miracle

Father Pernin looked for his house. It was nearly impossible to find; the streets had mostly disappeared. Finally, he spotted what was left of the shovel he'd used Sunday night. When he dug, though, he found everything in the trunks destroyed: The intense heat had penetrated twelve inches beneath the surface of the ground.

The priest did get one piece of good news. As he was walking by the river, a member of his parish called out, "Father, do you know what has happened to your tabernacle?'

"'No, what is it?'

"'Come quickly then, and see. Oh! Father, it is a great miracle!'"

And there it was, the wooden container shining bright white in the midst of the blackened ruins. The wagon had overturned in the river, but somehow the tabernacle had been caught by the wind and landed on logs. Then it floated downstream out of the range of the fire.

Today, the tabernacle is on display at the Peshtigo Fire Museum. You can see a photo of it here: http://www.peshtigofiremuseum.com/.

Aftermath

Outside help for Peshtigo was slow to arrive. It might not have come at all except for Frances "Frank" Fairchild, the young wife of Wisconsin governor Lucius Fairchild. Her husband and top officials in Madison had gone to aid the city of Chicago in the aftermath of its fire.

However, when Mrs. Fairchild got a telegram about the tragedy in Peshtigo, she sprang into action. She learned of a railroad car filled with clothing and supplies destined for Chicago survivors. She decided to send it to Peshtigo instead. When she realized it didn't contain blankets, she rounded some up by asking for donations. She sent other supplies to Peshtigo, and also alerted her husband to return to handle the emergency in his own state.

People in the city of Green Bay set up a relief committee for Peshtigo. They asked for donations of money and supplies for people who'd lost everything: flour, cured meat, blankets, bedding, axes and farming tools, clothing, and building supplies.

William Ogden, who'd invested so much in the town, arrived at the end of October. He stayed in Peshtigo for two months, throwing himself into efforts to rebuild the sawmills, shops, and railway lines. The woodenware factory was never rebuilt.

Although the actual origin of the fire isn't known for sure, most blamed it on the careless actions of railroad crews, who would often pile logs beside new tracks and burn them, then move on without bothering to put out the flames.

Despite this, expansion of the railroad continued, and new tracks were laid from Peshtigo to Marinette and Menominee by December 1871. Residents who stayed on faced a cold Wisconsin winter, with the remaining members of families huddled together in farmhouses, subsisting on canned food donations.

* * *

What happened in Peshtigo on October 8, 1871, remains the deadliest fire in American history. Most estimates place the death toll between 1,200 and 2,000—and possibly more. Getting an exact count is especially hard because in addition to regular full-time residents, there were many temporary railroad workers, salespeople, and other visitors in Peshtigo at the time. It's thought that at least 800 people perished in the town itself, including many of the newly arrived young men Father Pernin had seen enjoying themselves at the tavern on Sunday evening.

People in Peshtigo continue to honor the memories of those who lost their lives in the tragedy. The Peshtigo Fire Museum is located on the site of Father Pernin's original church. As for Father Pernin himself, he rebuilt his churches and went on to serve parishes in neighboring Minnesota as well. One of his first churches there was struck by lightning. The priest survived that too. He died in 1909 at age eighty-seven.

More on the Great Midwest Fires of 1871

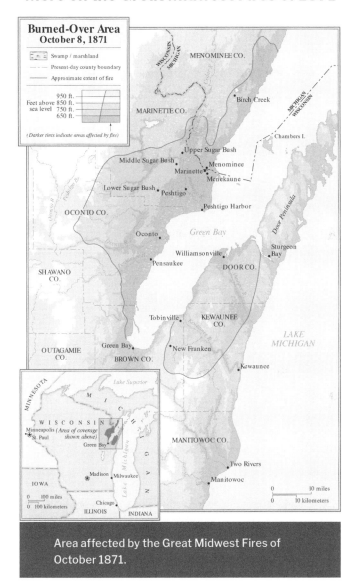

Area affected by the Great Midwest Fires of October 1871.

The Great Midwest Fires of 1871 spread over 2,400 square miles. More than a million acres burned. Along with Chicago and Peshtigo, the disaster affected other places too. The National Weather Service estimates as many as five hundred people died in Michigan; in Chicago, three hundred lives were lost and 17,000 buildings destroyed. To read more, visit: https://www.weather.gov/grb /peshtigofire2.

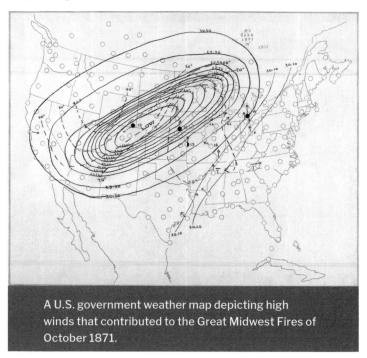

A U.S. government weather map depicting high winds that contributed to the Great Midwest Fires of October 1871.

The fires had several causes. In Peshtigo, these included poor forest management practices, such as burning downed trees and brush along new railroad tracks. Drought combined with high winds made the fires worse.

To better understand how weather contributed to the disaster, the National Weather Service examined records made by weather observers in 1871. Scientists noticed a low-pressure system over the central plains, which produced strong southwesterly winds. (A low-pressure system is a whirling mass of air that often produces rainstorms. But its leading edge can bring strong southwesterly winds. These winds can dry and heat fuels such as forests or wooden buildings and allow fires to spread.)

In the fall of 1871, along with warm temperatures and a lack of rain during the previous three months, these winds helped fuel the massive blazes in Peshtigo and Chicago, where many buildings were made of wood.

When fighting wildfires today, forest managers and fire experts monitor weather conditions with the help of **meteorologists**, scientists who study weather. But even modern tools like computers and weather satellites can't prevent all fire disasters. As we'll find out in Part Three, a warming climate, population growth, and the push for development are all adding new challenges to how we understand—and live with—fire in the twenty-first century.

CHAPTER FIVE

Chicago 1871: A Bigger Story

An 1871 illustration entitled *The Burning of Chicago*.

About the same time Father Peter Pernin was desperately digging in his garden as fire roared toward Peshtigo, another blaze erupted 250 miles to the south. Chicago, of course, was not an isolated North Woods village, but a major city. And the Great Chicago Fire, which burned almost three square miles and destroyed thousands of buildings, was destined to be the bigger story.

Chicago had been growing fast, from fewer than 5,000 people in 1840 to more than 300,000 thirty years later. The city was a hub for rail transportation, shipping, and industry. Its location on Lake Michigan was ideal. The Erie Canal connected Chicago to the East Coast. Branches of the Chicago River flowed through the city, and a canal provided access to the Mississippi River.

Chicago became known for its massive stockyards and meatpacking plants. The city boasted factories making everything from clothing to wagons, from bricks to farm equipment. The prospect of jobs attracted a growing population of German and Irish immigrants.

A devastating fire here would send shock waves across the whole country—and that's exactly what happened. So, while Peshtigo is often forgotten, there's a good chance you've heard about Mrs. O'Leary's cow kicking over a lantern to start the Great Chicago Fire. There's even an old song about it.

> *Late one night, when we were all in bed,*
> *Old Mother Leary left a lantern in the shed,*
> *and when the cow kicked it over, she winked her*
>   *eye and said,*
> *"There'll be a HOT time on the old town*
>   *tonight."*
> *FIRE, FIRE, FIRE!*

But is this how the fire began? To investigate, let's go back in time once more, to Sunday evening, October 8, 1871.

Milk Cows in the City

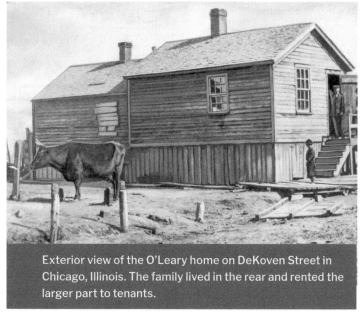

Exterior view of the O'Leary home on DeKoven Street in Chicago, Illinois. The family lived in the rear and rented the larger part to tenants.

Irish immigrants Catherine and Patrick O'Leary lived on DeKoven Street on Chicago's West Side. It was a neighborhood of unpaved streets and wooden cottages, dotted with sheds and small barns. Catherine and Patrick and their five children crowded into two rooms at the back of their house and rented out the front. Catherine helped support her family by selling milk. She kept several cows, a calf, and a horse to pull the milk wagon. On that October night, the barn was especially full: A load of fresh hay had recently been delivered.

Like Peshtigo, Chicago had been plagued by a long spell of warm, dry weather. Also like Peshtigo, Chicago was a tinderbox. Weary city firefighters had been scrambling to keep up with the blazes. Just the night before, a large fire had broken out in a mill next to a cardboard box factory, dangerously close to lumberyards piled high with dry pine.

And then came that windy Sunday. About eight o'clock that evening, the O'Leary family went to bed. Catherine had to be up at four the next morning to milk her cows. A neighbor named Daniel Sullivan later reported he saw flames erupting from the O'Leary barn about nine o'clock. Daniel banged on the door to wake the sleeping family.

Then he and another neighbor, Dennis Regan, turned their attention to the burning barn. Daniel is credited with saving the calf. Friends and neighbors rushed to the scene, and managed to keep the O'Leary's house from burning by dumping bucket after bucket of water on it.

But already the fire was on the move. All the elements of the fire triangle were present: heat from the air and fire, strong winds off the prairie, and a city crammed with wooden buildings—fuel—as dry as the wooden slash in the forests outside of Peshtigo that very same night.

A Young Reporter on the Scene

Our first eyewitness to the Chicago fire is Joseph Edgar "Ed" Chamberlin. Ed began his career in newspapers at the age of seventeen. In 1871, he was an eager twenty-year-old reporter for the *Chicago Evening Post.*

"I was at the scene in a few minutes," he wrote. "The land was thickly studded with one-story frame dwellings, cow-stables, pigsties, corn-cribs, sheds innumerable; every wretched building within four feet of its neighbor and everything of wood—not a brick or a stone in the whole area."

The fire was taking off fast. "I stepped in among some sheds south of Ewing Street; a fence by my side began to blaze," Ed wrote. "I beat a hasty retreat, and in five minutes the place where I had stood was all ablaze. Nothing could stop that conflagration there. It must sweep on until it reached a broad street, and then, everybody said, it would burn itself out."

Burn itself out? Not a chance.

About fifteen minutes after the blaze began, blacksmith William Lee, another neighbor of the O'Learys, ran to the neighborhood drugstore to turn in a fire alarm. Unlike Peshtigo, Chicago had a real fire department, with nearly two hundred firefighters and fire alarm boxes located throughout the city. Each alarm box had a switch inside that sent a signal to a telegraph operator at the fire department. The city also had horse-pulled steam fire engines, which could connect their fire hoses to hydrants to fight blazes.

Fire alarm box 296 was on the outside of a drugstore owned by Bruno Goll. While Goll later claimed to have sent in the alarm twice, the signals apparently never reached the command center. By the time the first horses and fire equipment arrived, the fire was fierce, hot, and impossible to control. Ed wrote, "Streams [of water] were thrown into the flame, and evaporated almost as soon as they struck it."

Historians point to a series of errors, communication lapses, and missteps that made a bad situation worse. Fire engines were sent to the wrong location, several fire companies close to the fire's origin weren't alerted, and reinforcements weren't called in until it was too late. The result was exactly what reporter Ed Chamberlin described: a fire out of control and moving relentlessly toward the center of the city.

Desperate Flight

Ed Chamberlin sprinted just ahead of the flames. He saw people spilling into the streets, dragging trunks or trying to carry valuables. The roads were soon clogged with wagons loaded with books, chairs, kitchenware, and other household items.

"All these things—the great, dazzling, mounting light, the crash and roar of the conflagration, and the desperate flight of the crowd—combined to make a scene of which no intelligent idea can be conveyed in words," wrote Ed.

Before long, the fire was attacking larger houses on more affluent streets. Here, Ed saw some people trying to rescue pianos. But there was little time. While these homes might look less likely to burn on the outside, inside

Chicago residents grabbed what they could as they fled the flames.

they had wooden floors, furniture, and walls. "Though mostly of brick, they ignited like tinder," Ed wrote.

"The wind had increased to a tempest, and hurled great blazing brands over our heads," Ed said. The gusts pushed the fire relentlessly, street after street, block after block, toward the main business district with its grand hotels, storefronts, and the courthouse.

The Glare of Fire

Near Courthouse Square, at about ten o'clock, a visitor from New York named Alexander Frear battled gusts as he left the six-story Sherman House hotel. He was in Chicago to visit family. Alexander's brother, a successful Chicago businessman, was out of town. But Alexander's sister-in-law was at home with three children, all under the age of fifteen. While not a reporter himself, Alexander later published an account of his experiences in a New York City newspaper.

The Sherman House hotel was destroyed by the 1871 fire. It was rebuilt and remained a popular destination until 1973.

"When I came down the wind was blowing fiercely through Clark Street to the river, and I had some difficulty in getting across the Courthouse square," he said. "I noticed the glare of the fire on the West Side as I came along, but thought nothing of it."

Alexander stopped to ask some men about the fire, but no one seemed to know much. "I kept on, but before I had reached the next street the cinders began to fall thick and fast all around me, and it was growing lighter all the time."

He then stepped into a bar to buy a cigar. "I don't think I was two minutes in the place, but when I came out the cinders were falling like snowflakes in every direction and lit the street, and there was a great hubbub of men and vehicles."

Clearly, the situation was growing worse. Eager to reach his brother's house, Alexander set off running, "but," he reported, "the walks were so crowded with people and the cinders were blown so thickly and fast that I found it was impossible."

He kept on. A woman carrying a bureau rammed him in the chest, breaking the crystal on his pocket watch. He held it in his hand and glanced at the time: It was now 11:30 p.m. As he stood there, a hot, live coal blew out of the sky and landed right on his palm.

When Alexander finally reached his relatives, he found his brother's wife frantically packing trunks with valuables, fearing that the house would burn. Quickly, the adults made plans. They decided that Alexander's sister-in-law and Mr. Wood, a friend and her husband's clerk, would wait for a wagon to move the family's prized possessions to safety.

Meanwhile, Alexander would take his nieces and nephew to the home of friends, the Kimballs, in a neighborhood they thought would be safer, out of the fire's path. Alexander hailed a horse-driven carriage and packed up the children. The youngest, Johnny, was an invalid, so Alexander carried him. The Kimballs were still sleeping and he had to ring the doorbell to wake them. He left his nieces and nephew there, then headed back on foot to his sister-in-law's house.

The scene was now more chaotic than before. It took Alexander more than an hour to get there. All the while, the fire was spreading relentlessly. When he got back to his brother's house, Alexander went up to the roof to try to figure out where the fire might be heading next.

It was hard to make out much with the smoke. But Alexander could tell the fire wasn't letting up. "Wherever I could see at all the wind blew the burning houses into a mass of live coals that was dazzling." Even more frightening, the fire was moving toward the Kimballs' neighborhood—right where Alexander had left his nieces and nephew.

Instead of being safe, the children were now in danger.

Alexander set out into the city once again, this time with his sister-in-law and Mr. Wood. They managed to hail a horse-drawn cab, but the streets were crammed, progress was slow, and the fire made a direct route impossible. Alexander said, "The roadway was full of people, and the din of voices and the melee of horses rendered unmanageable by the falling embers was terrible."

They kept asking people for news and learned the block where the Kimballs lived was now burning. The children's desperate mother jumped out of the cab and tried to run in that direction. They met an acquaintance who said the children had been taken to a certain hotel. They raced there next, but neither their friends nor the children could be found.

The adults split up again. Throughout that long night, Alexander was swept along in a fruitless search. The streets and sidewalks became clogged with abandoned possessions: toys, books, bedding, and musical instruments, all trampled underfoot. He saw other children, crying, separated and lost, but didn't find his nieces and nephew; he feared they had perished.

Daylight found Alexander near where he'd started out the evening before. The scene now was fiery chaos. "The Court-house, the Sherman House, the Tremont House, and the wholesale stores on Wabash Avenue, and the retail stores on Lake Street were now burning," said Alexander. "I was wet and scorched and bedraggled. My clothes were burnt full of holes on my arms and shoulders and back."

Fortunately, Alexander's ordeal had a happy ending. He reunited with his sister-in-law and Mr. Wood. His brother's house had been spared. Best of all, about four o'clock on Monday afternoon, word came that the children were safe.

We can only imagine what that night was like for

Alexander's nieces and nephew. But one thirteen-year-old girl who became separated from her family during the Great Chicago Fire *did* tell her story. Her name was Bessie Bradwell.

Historians estimate about three hundred people died in the Great Chicago Fire. The scope of damage horrified the nation, overshadowing the tragedy in Peshtigo.

CHAPTER SIX
A Storm of Falling Fire

Illustration of crowds trying to escape over the Randolph Street Bridge, which crosses the Chicago River in downtown Chicago.

A Storm of Falling Fire

Bessie Bradwell grew up in a family that loved reading and books, especially law books. Her father was Judge James B. Bradwell. Bessie's mother, Myra Bradwell, was an activist who fought for the right of women in Illinois to practice law. Myra was also the first woman in the United States to edit a legal publication: the *Chicago Legal News*.

On Sunday night, when the family realized the city was on fire, Bessie went with her dad to his office near Courthouse Square. Judge Bradwell hoped to save some precious law books, and he began packing up his collection. Meanwhile, Bessie's mother and her brother, Thomas, headed toward Lake Michigan for safety. Myra Bradwell carried their pet bird in a cage. It gasped for breath because of the smoke. (Incredibly, the bird survived!)

In her father's office, Bessie spotted one special book. It was a thick, heavy volume containing all the names and addresses of the subscribers to her mom's legal journal. She knew these records were important. (This was long before computers. There would be no easy way to replace the information.) So Bessie picked up this heavy book and said to her father, "'This is a good thing to save and I will take care of it.'"

And throughout the long ordeal to come, that's exactly what Bessie did.

Bessie on Her Own

Terrified residents seeking safety from the Chicago fire.

Since her father was still busy packing books, Bessie decided to head out to join her mother and brother.

Her father let her go. It's likely neither of them realized how quickly the fire was moving or how dangerous the situation had become.

On the street, Bessie was jostled by panicked crowds. To Alexander Frear, the whirling embers had seemed like burning rain, or a "storm of falling fire." Bessie put it this way: "It was like a snow storm only the flakes were red instead of white."

As Alexander Frear's story showed, it was easy for families to become separated on that chaotic night. And Bessie's tale might have turned out differently if she'd been caught alone in the crowds. But Bessie was lucky. Almost at once she found some friends.

"By chance, I met a gentleman and his wife, friends of my father and mother," Bessie recalled. "They said, 'Come right along with us,' and we proceeded down Washington St. toward the Lake."

A little while later, Bessie faced a choice. She could part from these friends to set out alone to find her mom and brother. Or she could stay with them and head in a different direction. She hesitated, but it seemed safer to remain with the adults.

Like Alexander Frear and reporter Ed Chamberlin, Bessie spent long hours that night trying to stay ahead of the shifting, terrifying flames. Several times, flying embers landed on her coat, and it began to burn.

"People would run up to me and smother the flames with their hands," Bessie remembered. "Then we hurried on, the fire madly pursuing us."

Finally, early on Monday morning, Bessie and her friends reached a safe area. They managed to find an open restaurant. It was crowded with survivors, all talking excitedly and sharing their experiences and remarkable stories of escape.

After breakfast, Bessie set out on her own to find her family. However, before leaving the restaurant, Bessie announced that if she wasn't able to reunite with her parents and brother for some reason, she would go stay with some former neighbors on the West Side.

Bessie's return journey turned out to be more difficult than she imagined. Many streets in the smoldering city were blocked off by police and firefighters. Some buildings were being dynamited on purpose to keep them from collapsing and hurting people. At one point, a police officer stopped Bessie and said it was too dangerous for her to go on.

Eventually, Bessie realized finding her family that day would be impossible. So she made her way to friends in their old neighborhood—all the while still carrying her mother's heavy book.

"To the Ends of the Earth"

Meanwhile, the night before, after Bessie had gone, her father had carried some of his books down to the street but couldn't find a cart or cab to carry them. It seemed too dangerous to wait any longer, so he abandoned his books and set off to join his family. He found his wife and son. But, to his astonishment, Bessie wasn't with them.

Bessie wrote later, "His first words were 'Where is Bessie?'

"Mother said, 'Why, I thought she was with you.'

"My father was sure I was dead. My mother, who was always an optimist, said, 'No, I'd trust that girl to go to the ends of the earth—she'll come out all right, don't you worry.'"

"Your Daughter Is Safe"

Bessie wasn't able to get home right away, and her father began to fear the worst. When he attended a citizens' meeting about the fire on Tuesday night, Judge Bradwell shared his heartbreak at the loss of his daughter. And he got a welcome surprise.

A man who'd seen Bessie at the restaurant on Monday morning cried, "Don't worry, Judge Bradwell, your daughter is safe on the west side and she carted that great heavy *Legal News* subscription book for nine hours.'"

All of Bessie's family (including the pet bird who lived a good long life) did come out all right. Not only that, Bessie's mother traveled out of town to find a printer so she could publish the next issue of her journal—right on time. In it, she appealed to lawyers around the country to send—you guessed it—law books to lawyers in Chicago who'd lost theirs.

As you might have predicted, Bessie grew up to become a lawyer. (Her brother did too.) Bessie later took over from her mom as editor of *Chicago Legal News*. Bessie lived from 1858 until 1927. Her mother, Myra Bradwell, was inducted into the National Women's Hall of Fame in 1994.

Get Out and Stay Out!

Many stories about fires of the past include people trying to save their possessions. But fire experts today have this advice in case of fire: *Get out and stay out!* In the event of a fire, the most important thing is to get out of a building quickly and safely—and not to stop to take anything with you or go back to get anything.

It's also important to have good communication. You might think that today Bessie could just keep in touch with her family by cell phone. But even if she and her parents had phones, cell service is often interrupted during a fire or natural disaster, such as a flood, earthquake, snowstorm, or hurricane.

That's why it's important to plan for emergencies in advance, not only for natural disasters, but where to meet up if you're separated from friends or adults in your family or group at a mall or a public event, like a parade. Be prepared!

Fannie Belle Becker: "I could not open my eyes"

Some people write about personal experiences right away. Others wait years. But you don't have to be grown up to tell your own story about something you have experienced.

Fannie Belle Becker was ten at the time of the Chicago Fire in 1871. She wrote about her experiences two years later. Part of her account appears here. You can find her entire story on this website: https://www.greatchicagofire.org/eyewitnesses /anthology-of-fire-narratives/.

As you read, you might notice some grammatical errors. That's because Fannie's account is an original, or **primary source.** This is how she wrote it. No one has made any corrections. Although you may notice unusual spelling, capital letters, or grammar, Fannie's voice shines right through. (Not all of her story is included here; places where sentences have been left out are marked with dots called ellipses.)

*   *   *

"Monday morning at three o'clock I was awakened and told to Dress for the Fire was all around us and we would soon be burnt out. . . . My ma put all her valubals into her sewing machine and locked it up and threw some things in her trunk . . . I carried . . . a little lady called Jennie . . . some of you may not know who little Jennie is so I will say that she is a little China doll a Christmas present when I was Five years old and I will always keep her as a Relic of the Chicago Fire. . . .

". . . we came to our friends brothers house we stayed here until the fire drove us out then the heat was so intense that it drove us down to the waters Edge and then my uncle who was with us (and, had arrived Saturday) took his hat and poured water on the things to keep them from burning but thousands and thousands of dollar's worth of goods were burned right there on the waters Edge. Although our things were saved we sat there until I was almost blind with the dirt and cinders that filled the air I could not open my eyes, so that when I walked ma had to lead me.

"I did not have anything to eat from Sunday afternoon until Monday afternoon at about four o'clock. Then we went out to the City limits on the South side to the house of a friend I stayed here two days and then I went out in the country with my cousins, and stayed there one week and then I came to Fruit-Port [Michigan]. . . . I almost went barefoot and without any good clothes. I was well treated and one of them even took off her over shoes and let me wear them that I might go out in the cold weather and play."

CHAPTER SEVEN
Aftermath: Chicago in Ruins

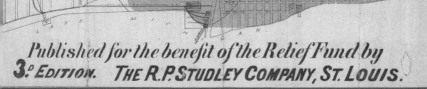

Map of the Burnt District in Chicago in 1871.

The Chicago fire destroyed more than 17,000 buildings.

Reporter Ed Chamberlin had been on the scene at the start of the Great Chicago Fire. And after hours of racing through the streets ahead of the flames, Ed was exhausted. Early Monday morning, he collapsed on a pile of wood in a lumberyard. Not the safest place to rest, but Ed was too tired to move.

Ed woke at dawn in the smoky air of a city still burning. "Then a curious-looking crimson ball came up out of the lake, which they said was the sun; but oh, how sickly and insignificant it looked!"

As he started home, Ed met young women on their way to work. "They saw the fire and smoke before them, but could not believe that the city, with their means of livelihood, had been swept away during that night."

The Burnt District, as it was called, extended about four miles long and two-thirds of a mile across. The fire struck the heart of the city, destroying more than 17,000 structures, including schools, hotels, newspaper buildings, stores, factories, and banks.

Since this was before computers, the loss of historical records and documents was especially severe. The most heartbreaking, perhaps, was Abraham Lincoln's original draft of the Emancipation Proclamation, which had been housed at the Chicago Historical Society.

Most historians put the number killed at about 300, far fewer than Peshtigo. However, more than 90,000 people were left homeless; even more lost their jobs or sources of livelihood. Housing and clean water were in short supply. Some survivors simply left town; others scrounged enough material to build temporary wooden shanties until they could rebuild.

Donations poured in after the fire, although people with wealth and means were able to rebuild their lives more quickly than others.

Back to Mrs. O'Leary's Cow

Early newspaper reports claimed the fire was caused by a cow kicking over a lantern while being milked. This wasn't a fact but a rumor, most likely begun by a reporter seeking to dramatize a story to sell newspapers.

The tale quickly took hold in the public imagination. However, Catherine O'Leary (and her children) always claimed she was sleeping when the fire began—and that she had not been careless and left a lantern in the barn. But a poor Irish immigrant was easy to blame, and although she was officially cleared in 1871, even today many people assume the legend is true.

That's not surprising, actually. Researchers tell us that unproven rumors, lies, and false information spread more quickly than facts. Rumors also can cause harm. Catherine O'Leary was treated as guilty for the rest of her life. Eventually, she refused to speak with reporters and the family sold their property and moved away.

In 1997, in a gesture of goodwill, the Chicago City Council passed a unanimous resolution to "forever exonerate Mrs. O'Leary and her cow from all blame in regard to the Great Chicago Fire of 1871." By that time, of course, Catherine was no longer around. She died in 1895.

Today, there's an emblem in Chicago marking the spot where the fire began. You can find it inside the Robert J. Quinn Fire Academy—a training center for firefighters.

The city of Chicago faced a major rebuilding challenge following the devastating fire of 1871.

Panorama of San Francisco after the earthquake and fire of 1906.

Part Two

THE TWENTIETH CENTURY
Fires That Shook America

CHAPTER EIGHT
Chicago 1903: The Iroquois Theater Fire

We'll stay in Chicago to examine our next fire, which took place in 1903, thirty-two years after the Great Fire. The Iroquois Theater fire didn't rage through the city. Instead, it took place in one building on a single afternoon—but cost twice as many lives as the 1871 disaster.

Chicago had rebuilt quickly after the Great Fire. By the time the new century arrived, the city's population had surged to more than a million, making it the second-largest American city after New York. The anniversary of the Great Fire was commemorated as "Chicago Day," a time to celebrate the city's remarkable recovery.

Chicago was becoming a modern city. It offered

residents and visitors many attractions, including music, theaters, and new department stores. With their lavish window displays, department stores attracted well-off shoppers, especially White women. Middle- and upper-class mothers could take their children shopping, have lunch at a nice restaurant, and then attend a matinee (afternoon) performance in Chicago's bustling theater district. Families from the outskirts could come in by train to enjoy a fun day in the big city.

To please these audiences, Chicago hosted touring productions—plays that had first been performed in New York. Moving a large production by train from place to place was expensive, and theaters in Chicago were under a lot of pressure to sell as many tickets as possible.

Selling tickets was definitely on the minds of the owners of a brand-new theater scheduled to open in time for the busy holiday season of 1903. The Iroquois Theater on Randolph Street, the "Broadway of Chicago," did manage to open its doors on November 23. But that rush would have deadly consequences.

A Crowded Performance

Bryan Foy had just turned seven when his dad, the famous actor and comedian Eddie Foy, snared him a free pass to see the Iroquois Theater's first production, *Mr. Bluebeard*, a musical comedy for families, inspired by an old folktale.

Bryan's dad was the star attraction for this lavish production, which featured more than 150 actors, singers, and dancers. The people, props, costumes, and elaborate scenery filled twelve railroad cars. Many of the scenery backdrops were curtains made of canvas or thin, gauzy material—material that might easily catch fire, especially under hot stage lights.

A festive holiday crowd gathered for the performance on Wednesday afternoon, December 30, 1903. The gorgeous new theater had seats for 1,724; a standing-room ticket cost thirty-five cents. There were at least 200 people standing; 300 cast and crew members worked or waited backstage. Altogether, around 2,300 people crowded into the theater that day.

Before the end of the afternoon, 602 would lose their lives.

A Marble Palace

Eddie Foy was a hometown success story. He'd started his career in Chicago and gained fame in New York as a comic actor and singer. He'd brought his wife and four children on tour (there would eventually be seven Foy children who performed together). They were staying at the Sherman House, which had been rebuilt after the big fire and was only a block from the theater.

The theater was absolutely beautiful; Eddie said later it reminded him of a marble palace. The interior was festooned with draperies of crimson. It featured a grand staircase with columns and archways. Two thousand light bulbs glimmered like stars in the ceiling. On the main level, nineteen rows of seats could accommodate more than seven hundred patrons. The theater boasted two balconies: the dress circle and, above that, the gallery, or second balcony.

Not only was it beautiful, the Iroquois Theater was proclaimed to be absolutely fireproof. "We were told that the theater was the very last word in efficiency, convenience, and most important of all, safety," said Eddie.

In fact, the Iroquois Theater was anything but safe.

"Something Deadly Wrong"

"We drew big crowds all through Christmas week," Eddie Foy recalled. "On Wednesday, December 30, at the bargain-price matinee, the house was packed, and many were standing."

The audience was full of students, teachers, mothers, and many shopworkers who'd gotten the afternoon off. "It struck me as I looked out over the crowd during the first act that I had never seen so many women and children in the audience," Eddie Foy said.

It was so full, there wasn't an empty seat for Bryan, so Eddie said he had to "stow him wherever I could." That turned out to be a stool off to the right of the stage, near where an electrician ran the lighting switchboard.

The first act went smoothly; the second act began a little before three o'clock. At about that time, Eddie was in his dressing room getting ready for his next skit, in which he would appear as a comical character called Sister Anne. He wore a pigtailed wig, flowered hat, long dress, and pantaloons. He performed with actors who wore an elephant costume. The act was designed to get laughs.

Eddie would go on after a song-and-dance number, "In the Pale Moonlight," which called for the theater to be dark except for stage lights. As the singers, dancers, and musicians began, trouble erupted backstage. A flash of sparks flew out from a strong, hot, blue floodlight. The sparks ignited a swaying canvas curtain, and flame shot up into other curtains.

Stagehands started to beat the flames out and pour chemical powders on them. At the theater's light switchboard, in the wings near where Bryan sat, an electrician tried to flip a switch to turn on the theater's lights. Instead, part of a burning curtain fell on the switchboard, and no lights came on.

Inside his dressing room, Eddie heard some commotion. He ignored it at first, but the noise grew louder. "I jerked my door open, and instantly I knew there was something deadly wrong. It could be nothing else but fire!"

As smoke billowed from the stage, audience members also started to sense something was wrong. At first, the dancers kept performing and the musicians continued to play, hoping to keep people calm. Eddie ran to find Bryan. "Probably not 40 seconds had elapsed since I heard the first commotion—but already the terror was beginning."

"Take My Boy Out!"

Eddie grabbed Bryan and rushed toward a rear door. Suddenly, he stopped short, haunted by the thought of so many children in the audience. He hardly looked like a figure of authority in his silly costume. Even so, Eddie felt he had to try to prevent a panicked stampede.

"'Take my boy out!'" Eddie shouted, tossing Bryan into the arms of the nearest stagehand. He watched them get to the rear doors. Then Eddie strode onto center stage.

"'Take your time, folks. . . . Go slow, people! You'll get out,'" he called loudly. Although desperately worried about his son, Eddie made a special effort to speak slowly and calmly. It didn't seem, though, that anyone was listening. Already, he could see people in the balconies surging to escape.

Eddie couldn't figure out why the theater's fireproof curtain hadn't been lowered, and hollered at stagehands to get it down. This asbestos curtain was supposed to prevent fires in the stage area from spreading into the auditorium. But the curtain had snagged partway down; the stagehand in charge was nowhere to be found.

As he looked out into the audience, Eddie saw nothing but chaos. It didn't seem to him as if the ushers had ever practiced a fire drill (they hadn't). Backstage, it was just as chaotic. There wasn't even a fire alarm box in the theater that connected to the fire department. Someone had to run down the street to call in the alarm.

One last musician was still valiantly playing the violin in the orchestra pit below Eddie. Suddenly, as performers and stagehands fled out the rear doors, a draft of cold winter air rushed into the theater. You remember the fire triangle: heat, fuel, and an oxidizing agent. The burst of air caused a tremendous surge of fire—right over Eddie's head.

"Then came a cyclonic blast of fire from the stage out into the auditorium . . . A huge billow of flame leaped out past me and over me and seemed to reach even to the balconies." Eddie's wig started to smolder. He could no longer be heard over the screams. There was nothing more he could do.

"But by this time, the inferno behind me was so terrible that I wondered whether I could escape that way . . . I hesitated momentarily, but Bryan had gone out by the rear—if he had gone out at all—and I was irresistibly drawn to follow, that I might learn his fate more quickly," said Eddie.

"As I rushed out of the theater, I could think of nothing but my boy," said Eddie, who never shook off the horror of that day. "I became more and more frightened; as I neared the street, I was certain he hadn't got out.

"But when I reached the sidewalk and looked around wildly, there he was with his faithful friend [the stagehand], just outside the door. I seized him in my arms and turned toward the hotel. At that moment I longed only to see my family all together and to thank God that we were all still alive."

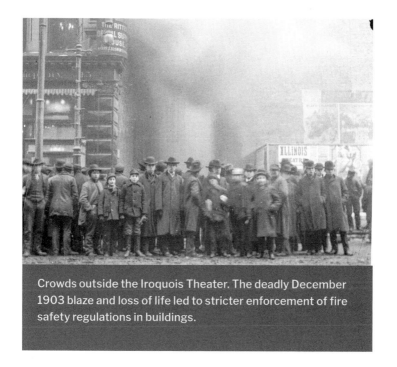

Crowds outside the Iroquois Theater. The deadly December 1903 blaze and loss of life led to stricter enforcement of fire safety regulations in buildings.

Serious Safety Violations

Once firefighters arrived, they were able to put the fire out quickly, but that did little to prevent the severe loss of life in those first few moments. Investigations revealed numerous safety violations that led to the horrific death toll. Corners had been cut in the rush to open.

For example, the theater should have had a sprinkler

Interior of the Iroquois Theater in Chicago after the deadly fire of December 30, 1903. A fireball, propelled by a cold blast of air from the rear doors behind the stage, flew into the theater, killing many in the two balconies who could not escape in time.

system, but didn't. The theater wasn't equipped with firefighting equipment, such as axes to break open doors, or even buckets of water to dowse small fires from lights that malfunctioned. Some fire exit signs were hidden by drapes; many of the ushers didn't know how to work the handles on the emergency exit doors.

Despite all this, the theater had been given the okay

to open. Why? Most historians think it was a combination of corruption and greed. The building approval system put profits first, and theater owners used their influence to get inspectors to overlook violations.

The result was tragedy. Hundreds of people, mostly in the balconies, died within ten minutes of the fire blast. Others were trampled by stampeding crowds.

The death toll was 602; 420 were women and just under 200 were children.

The fire sent shock waves rippling across the theater world. Chicago, as well as other major cities from New York to London, passed stronger fire safety regulations for theaters. Some policies were changed, such as not locking theater doors. The following year a company developed a special door with a push bar, or panic bar, to make it easier for people to escape a burning public building. A version of it is still used today.

Eddie Foy continued to perform until 1923, five years before he passed away. As for Eddie's son Bryan, he followed his dad into show business. Bryan performed with his family in a stage act called "Eddie Foy and the Seven Little Foys." He went on to a successful career as a film producer and director. His many credits include a Nancy Drew film series, based on the books about the young detective.

Today's building codes are much stronger than they were back in 1903. Nevertheless, it's always important to take fire safety seriously.

Pay attention when you practice fire drills in school. Also, get in the habit of being aware of your surroundings. For example, when you enter a sports arena, gym, or theater, take a moment to look around you. Where are the lighted exit signs? You should be able to spot them even when the main lights are dimmed. When you do, remember that buildings are safer now because of tragic events like the Iroquois Theater fire so long ago.

LEARN NOT TO BURN

The National Fire Protection Association (NFPA), https://www.nfpa.org/, was established in 1896. NFPA is a global nonprofit organization dedicated to preventing injuries, death, and destruction from fires. It provides information about fire safety codes and also sponsors Fire Prevention Week. NFPA offers fire safety tips for kids (and adults) in their LEARN NOT TO BURN program.

Tip sheets are available in more than a dozen languages. The sheets include information about how smoke alarms work and good practices to follow whenever you or someone else is cooking. For instance, you should always stay in the kitchen when frying food or cooking with grease. There's also a tip sheet on how to make a fire escape plan. You or a grown-up reading this book with you can find a list of tip sheets in English and other languages at https://www.nfpa.org/Public-Education/Teaching-tools/Safety-tip-sheets/Easy-to-read-handouts-in-other-languages.

You can also find fun activities by visiting the website for the NFPA mascot, Sparky the Fire Dog: http://www.sparky.org. Here you can learn even more about fire safety, such as remembering to stay three feet away from anything that can get hot, making sure your home has a working smoke alarm, knowing the sound a smoke alarm makes, and practicing fire escape plans.

Six Months Later: Another Deadly Fire for Families

Just six months later, on June 15, 1904, more than 1,300 people from the Lower East Side in New York City boarded the steamship *General Slocum*. The boat had been chartered for a special church picnic and outing. Most of the families were immigrants from Germany. A fire broke out on board soon after the boat started up the East River, leading to the deaths of 1,021 innocent people, many of them children.

An investigation found that many safety regulations had been ignored. The life preservers were old and crumbling. Crew members were poorly trained. The captain was accused of poor judgment in not getting the boat to shore quickly enough. He was tried and found guilty of criminal negligence and served time in jail. The disaster led to an effort to reinspect passenger steamers and set new regulations for fire extinguishers, fire hoses, and life preservers.

Despite the high death toll, the *General Slocum* fire is not well known, perhaps because it affected

The fire on the steamship *General Slocum* cost more than 1,000 lives.

many poor immigrant families. But prior to the 9/11 attack in 2001, the *General Slocum* fire was the greatest loss of life of any New York City disaster. If you live in or visit New York City, you can find a memorial to the victims in Tompkins Square.

CHAPTER NINE
San Francisco 1906: Double Disaster

Houses in San Francisco were damaged both by the April 18, 1906, earthquake and the fires that followed.

"Wednesday morning, April 18, I was awakened by a slight shaking," twelve-year-old Elsie Cross wrote to her friend Ruth.

"Now as earthquakes are usually gentle and mild I waited for it to pass away. Instead of that it began to wrench and by that time I was in my doorway. (That being considered the safest place.) Then it began to just go up and down as a cat shakes a rat and I, thinking the world was coming to an end, said a prayer and waited for results. . . .

"After we got out of the house my father said that the only trouble now, was fire. All that day there were shocks and the sun was a ball of purply red from the smoke. It was very hot."

Elsie and her family were living through a horrific double disaster. It began when an **earthquake** struck San Francisco, California, at 5:12 a.m. on April 18, 1906. The city sits on a peninsula between the Pacific Ocean and San Francisco Bay. In 1906, about 450,000 people lived there.

The earthquake lasted sixty-five seconds, causing

severe and immediate damage. (Today, experts estimate it was a 7.8 magnitude on the **Richter scale**. For more about measuring earthquakes, see the special section titled "Measuring Earthquakes" on page 108.)

Walls and chimneys toppled; roads buckled and ruptured; structures near the waterfront sank into sandy, wet soil. Many small fires broke out across the city from overturned candles or lamps, or leaks from gas stoves and pipes.

The city did have an excellent telegraph fire alarm system and forty-two horse-drawn fire engines. However, the water system was outdated, with small pipes and not enough pressure to pump water from reservoirs or the bay. Some water hydrants worked; others did not. The earthquake also damaged many streets and made fighting the fire difficult.

To make matters worse, the city's chief fire engineer, Dennis Sullivan, was fatally injured in the earthquake itself and died a few days later. Would things have turned out differently if Chief Sullivan had been there to lead firefighting efforts over the next three days? No one can say for sure. But as historian Andrea Rees

Rescuing people from the rubble in San Francisco.

Davies noted, "The low water supply and lack of central command made a deadly combination."

As fires spread, they merged. The smoke was visible for miles. "Within an hour after the earthquake shock the smoke of San Francisco's burning was a lurid tower visible a hundred miles away," said the writer Jack London, who rushed in from his ranch forty miles away to cover the disaster for a magazine. "And for three days and nights this lurid tower swayed in the sky, reddening the sun, darkening the day, and filling the land with smoke."

The fire was difficult to stop. When firefighters made a stand against the blaze in one place, other fires came from behind or the sides. Firefighters tried using dynamite to create firebreaks to control the flames. However, Chief Sullivan was the dynamite expert and he wasn't there. As a result, sometimes the explosives sent embers flying, starting new fires and making the situation worse.

The smoke from the San Francisco fire billowed high into the sky and was visible miles away.

Over three days, the San Francisco earthquake and fire destroyed more than four and a half square miles, 28,000 buildings, and more than five hundred city blocks, including most of the main business area and San Francisco's thriving Chinatown district. It's estimated that about 80 percent of the city was affected.

While an accurate death toll isn't known, historians believe at least 3,000 people died and at least 200,000 lost their homes, including Elsie Cross and her family. More than a century later, it's still considered one of the deadliest natural disasters in American history.

"As Bright as Day"

Elsie Cross wrote about her experience soon after escaping the city. Elsie's family lived in the Western Addition, a San Francisco neighborhood to the west of a wide boulevard called Van Ness Avenue. As the fires spread, Elsie's parents realized it wouldn't be safe to remain where they were.

"Wednesday afternoon with a few blankets, a canvas, and an eiderdown we went way out in the Sunset where the fire could never reach & slept part of the night on the front doorsteps," Elsie wrote to her friend.

The Sunset District is just south of Golden Gate Park, where many sought safety. That night, the light from fires made it "as bright as day," Elsie said. She and her brother fell asleep, but her parents kept watch.

"The next day in the morning [Thursday, the second day of the three-day fire] my mother & father & I packed in a steamer trunk old family laces, miniatures, & clothing. In the afternoon my father drove us in his buggy & we put the silver, jewelry, family pictures, & blankets in . . ." Elsie wrote to her friend a few weeks later from the city of Oakland. Elsie felt sorry to leave her piano behind, "but as nothing else could be done I did not say anything."

Elsie's family had lost their home. But reading her letter, a primary source, we can also see that the Crosses were fairly well-off. This was a White family that seemed to be living in a comfortable way. For example, they had silver and jewelry and could afford a piano. They also owned a buggy, which made it much easier for them to leave—and save at least some of their valuable possessions. It wouldn't be easy for Elsie and her family to rebuild their lives, of course. But they were at least able to start with something, unlike other families who lost everything.

And for many other San Francisco residents, escaping with even the clothes on their backs would turn out to be a harrowing and dangerous ordeal.

African American families during the earthquake and fire. Many Black families lived in the hard-hit downtown area and lost their homes.

MEASURING EARTHQUAKES

An earthquake occurs when two blocks of Earth's surface suddenly slip past each other. The surface where they slip is called a **fault**. Scientists now know the San Francisco earthquake was caused by a rupture of 296 miles on the **San Andreas fault**.

The first warning happened at 5:12 a.m. on Wednesday, April 18, 1906, with a **foreshock**, a smaller earthquake that occurs first. About twenty seconds later, violent and intense shaking erupted, lasting sixty-five seconds. The **epicenter,** or point of the eruption, was near San Francisco, but the quake was felt as far away as southern Oregon, Los Angeles, and central Nevada.

Today, we use the Richter scale, a measurement developed in 1935 by Charles Richter, to indicate the magnitude of an earthquake. Although that scale hadn't yet been developed in 1906, scientists

Souvenir hunters in the rubble. Fears of panic and looting led the mayor of San Francisco to declare martial law. This brought soldiers in to patrol the city. The mayor's declaration went to the extreme, calling for looters to be shot. Some people protested the order and complained about the troops. Troops stayed until early July and are credited with helping in relief efforts. You can read more about martial law during the disaster at https://www.nps.gov/prsf /learn/historyculture/1906-earthquake-law-enforcement.htm.

have estimated the San Francisco earthquake's intensity to be 7.8 on a scale where 9.0 is a great earthquake bringing total destruction.

Although the 1906 earthquake didn't lead to immediate major changes in building codes, it did spur the first large study on earthquakes and the San Andreas fault.

SEE ELSIE CROSS'S LETTER—THEN WRITE ONE

Along with diaries, newspapers, and journals, letters are another way to learn about the past—and record your own experiences.

You can see Elsie's letter yourself at the California Historical Society, which mounted a 2019 special online exhibit by librarian Frances Kaplan, entitled "Children's Voices from the Archives: Remembering the 1906 earthquake and fire." https://californiahistoricalsociety.org/blog /childrens-voices-from-the-archives-remembering -the-1906-earthquake-and-fire/.

Now try writing a letter about something that's happened to you. It doesn't have to be as dramatic as surviving a huge earthquake, though. You could pretend to write to someone from the past and try to describe what it's like to watch television or use a computer. Or you could describe a trip to the store or something you like to do with a friend. Since much of this book is about forests, you might try to write a letter to someone far away describing the trees in your town or city.

CHAPTER TEN
Fire on Our Faces

Elsie Cross wrote about her experiences just weeks after being shaken by the San Francisco earthquake on that April morning. Our next eyewitness, Lily Soo Hoo Sung, told her story about escaping the city during the fire in an interview many years later. Even so, her memories are vivid.

Hearing many voices (and there is a link at the end of this chapter you can follow to actually listen to Mrs. Sung's voice) is vital, and helps us to better understand the past and how events affected people who lived at the time. Is there someone whose story you want to learn about and preserve?

Some Background for Lily's Story

Lily was born on April 16, 1899; the earthquake struck just two days after her seventh birthday. Her father served as the minister of a Chinese Presbyterian church, a Protestant church. We know that her family believed in education. Lily's eldest brother was away at college, and Lily herself would later graduate from college. In 1906, she and her six other brothers and sisters lived with their parents in Chinatown, a thriving district of about 25,000 people.

During the 1800s, men from China had come to California to work in the Gold Rush and on the railroads. These immigrants toiled extraordinarily hard, determined to send money home to support their families in China. But the conditions in which they lived and worked in America were exceedingly harsh. They were treated badly and faced extreme prejudice.

Then, in 1882, the United States Congress passed the Chinese Exclusion Act. This law prevented workers from China from coming to America for most jobs. The Chinese Exclusion Act is one example of America's history of hostility toward people of color. It is also the only law in our history that targeted people from a single ethnic or national background and prevented them from immigrating to the United States.

Knowing this enables us to better see how racial prejudice affected Lily's family and community during this natural disaster. In the early hours of the San Francisco fire, White officials forced Chinatown residents to leave their homes. However, firefighting resources were put elsewhere. There was no chance for families to save their household goods. All of Chinatown was destroyed by dynamiting.

Historian Andrea Rees Davies has studied the disaster and relief efforts in 1906. She found that the city didn't care about helping Chinatown families. "As the few surviving records suggest, the men responsible for firefighting were not concerned with saving this neighborhood."

Dr. Davies's research also shows that people of Chinese heritage continued to be treated unfairly during the relief and rebuilding efforts. Dr. Davies explains that "San Francisco's earthquake and fires exposed social inequalities but did not eliminate them."

When we read Lily's story with this in mind, we can better imagine how frightening it must have been to be swept up in a crowd and thrown together with strangers who might treat her and her family cruelly. Lily and her siblings survived—thanks to resilience, determination, and love for one another.

But their journey to safety was not an easy one.

"We Were Pushed Up the Hill"

Early on Wednesday morning, Lily woke when the house started to shake violently. Her favorite doll fell to the floor and its pretty porcelain head broke. "The week before we had gone on a picnic, and we had caught polliwogs . . . and we had them in this jar and all the polliwogs were on the floor and the glass container was broken," she remembered.

Lily's parents stayed calm. But word soon came that they would have to leave. Lily's father called together some of his church members who lived nearby to make plans. Neighbors and the family split into smaller groups with the goal of taking a ferry out of the city, across the bay to Oakland.

Lily's fourteen-year-old sister Clara took charge of one group, which included Lily, a younger brother and sister, ages five and three, and a neighbor. In her account of the fire, Lily didn't give the woman's name. She did remember that their neighbor had a hard time walking because her feet had been bound as a girl. (The practice of foot binding to make a woman's feet smaller was banned in China in 1912.)

Lily's mother had thrown together a sack for Clara to carry. It contained a change of clothing for each child, a loaf of bread, and a glass bottle of water. Almost from the start, Clara, Lily, and the others were caught up in a crush of people, as officials drove thousands of residents out of Chinatown. There was no way to escape the press of the surging throng.

Lily recalled that "there were crowds pushing up along the street so we were pushed up the hill. We were supposed to go down to the ferry to go to Oakland, but then there were so many people trying to get away from the fire, so they thought the thing to do was to go up. So we got pushed up, up, up and sometimes it wasn't very easy to get around these places that the houses had all fallen down.

"We could feel the fire on our faces, even several blocks away. My sister tried to keep us away from the fire 'cause we were walking so slowly because of this lady [their neighbor] . . . and we could feel the warmth of the fire on our faces," Lily said.

They walked past houses so damaged by the earthquake that Lily could look right inside, the way you can see into a dollhouse. The crowd kept pushing Lily and her family the wrong way: up the hill rather than to the ferry dock. But there was simply no way they could break free to turn around.

San Francisco's business district looking upward toward the Fairmont Hotel. Buildings with steel frames fared better in the earthquake. Today, renovations to historic buildings constructed before 1906 often require extensive upgrades to improve earthquake safety.

It was also hard to keep together, but Clara was determined not to lose any of her younger siblings. She knew it might be impossible to find a little child again in the crowd. Lily remembered, "So sister said, 'no matter what happens, stay real still, and I'll come back and get you.'

"So that's what we did. And we didn't have very much to eat. Part way, this lady, the one with the bound feet, fell against my sister, and she dropped the sack with the bottle of water, and the bread was all soaked. That was the first time I ever saw her [Clara] cry."

When this happened, some people near them started to laugh. Lily never forgot this cruel and heartless response. "Here was the water all broken, nothing to eat, nothing to drink, and being pushed up the hill." How could anyone make fun of them and laugh about it?

Even though Lily was only seven, she did her best to help Clara and protect her little brother and sister. "At nighttime we had no place to sleep or to rest. . . . We couldn't really lie down, but we sat as well as we could. See, I had a little brother and a little sister, and they hung on tightly to me. And they were such good children," Lily recalled.

"They didn't cry even when they were knocked down, 'cause these crowds pushing us . . . you know, would knock us down. I was seven. I felt quite responsible and quite a big sister. So they would not cry, but they'd look up tearfully at me and hold my hand closer."

In this desperate rush of refugees, it took Lily and her siblings two days to make their way down to the ferry building by the bay. By then the place was packed with people trying to escape. Even so, being away from the crowded, dangerous streets was the first time Lily felt even a tiny bit safe.

Finally, they got across the bay on a ferry. In Oakland, disaster relief volunteers were passing out coffee and donuts to the refugees. Lily would always remember that too. It was the first real food she'd had in days. "And, oh my, that tasted so good." For the rest of her life, the smell of hot coffee brought that moment back.

Meanwhile, the rest of the family had also managed to get to Oakland. Lily's father had been sending members of his church to look for them among the new arrivals. Lily said, "And they finally found us and took us back to our parents.

"And they were so happy, and we were so happy. I can remember mother with tears streaming down her face, and father just holding us so close."

A resident of Chinatown walks among the ruins of the community.

Lily's family didn't go back to San Francisco. They stayed in Oakland, later moving to Berkeley, where she went to high school. Lily went on to lead a remarkable life. She attended Oberlin College and served as vice president of the Chinese Students' Alliance. After graduation, Lily married educator William Sung and moved to Shanghai, where she taught for a time at Shanghai University. The couple had four children and later returned to the United States. Lily died in 1993 at age ninety-four.

Read more and hear Lily Sung's voice

- Lily's interview by Connie Young Yu is part of the Chinese Historical Society of America. You can read her entire story and see photos at https://www.chsa .org/wp-content/uploads/2013/04/Lily-Sung.pdf.
- You can hear Lily and other survivors in a 2006 National Public Radio feature on the 100th anniversary of the San Francisco fire. Visit: https://www .npr.org/templates/story/story.php?storyId=5343414.

Remains of the Chinatown arch in San Francisco.

Fire on Our Faces

Child refugees after the earthquake and fire. Lily and her family escaped to Oakland. Families of Chinese heritage who stayed in San Francisco were separated into their own refugee camp because of prejudice.

African American children in one of the refugee camps set up after the disaster. Most of San Francisco's neighborhoods were primarily White at this time, except Chinatown. Many Black families lived in the downtown area devastated by the fire.

John the Rat-Catcher

Like Lily Sung, John J. Conlon was seven at the time of the 1906 fire. His account of the disaster includes his work afterward catching rats! Since bubonic plague is often spread to humans from bacteria carried by the fleas of infected rats, reducing the rat population helped prevent a serious epidemic. (You can read more about bubonic plague in *The Deadliest Diseases Then and Now*.)

"There was a bubonic plague scare shortly after the fire and because the fleas on rats were carriers of the germs, the city paid a bounty for dead rats," said John. "These payments were my introduction to the functions of the 'middle man.'

"An older lad enriched himself by paying the neighborhood youngsters with candy for dead rats that he exchanged for cash at the repaired Emergency Hospital. The fire drove thousands of rats into our district and Mother was horrified by them. Consequently, to avoid attracting them, all were instructed to securely cover garbage cans.

"Every morning, after the women had deposited the breakfast trash in the cans, I would remove the covers. Returning in about an hour, I would inspect the galvanized cans and if any rats were trapped therein, cans were tipped so that my Fox Terrier could kill the emerging rodent; then to the middle man for candy."

CHAPTER ELEVEN

New York 1911: The Triangle Fire

The Asch Building, scene of the Triangle factory fire in New York City on March 25, 1911.

Five years after the San Francisco disaster, a horrific fire in New York City shocked Americans into confronting issues of injustice in the workplace. It brought attention to the voices of working people, especially young women immigrants laboring for long hours at low pay.

It happened on Saturday afternoon, March 25, 1911, at the Triangle Waist Company. This was a factory located in the Asch Building near Washington Square. Here, the five hundred workers, mostly young immigrant Jewish women, made popular blouses called shirtwaists. (They looked like a men's white dress shirt.)

It was nearly closing time. We can imagine the sewing machine operators were eagerly awaiting the end of another long, fifty-two-hour workweek. It was payday too. In the late afternoon, Anna Pidone, a factory forelady, began to distribute pay envelopes on the ninth floor, where the women and girls were still busy on 278 sewing machines.

"We went from machine to machine and gave out the pay envelopes," said Anna. When that was done, "I went over near the freight elevator where the button was and rang the bell for everybody to stop work at 4:45, [as] that was the end of the day.

"I didn't know there was a fire and I went to the dressing room. Suddenly someone ran to the dressing room and cried 'Fire.' I came out of the dressing room and saw everything was in flames. I ran to the front door and the door was locked. Many people began to go to the windows to jump from the windows," Anna said later. By that time, Anna remembered, "The fire danced on the machines."

Anna hollered for her sister, who worked there too, but couldn't find her. The room had now filled with smoke. Anna ran to a window and looked down at the street, nine floors below. It was too far to jump. So Anna looked for another escape route. She remembered a back staircase near the freight elevator. This door was open, and Anna got down to the street safely.

The Triangle fire likely started in a pile of scrap material and then spread rapidly—so rapidly that many workers were trapped. Although there were rules against it, some of the factory doors had been locked. Many believed this was done deliberately to prevent workers from stealing. The fire escape was useless and didn't lead to safety. And firefighters' ladders didn't reach high enough.

Anna was one of the lucky ones. But 146 others, almost all young women, including her sister, perished that day in a tragedy that shocked America.

The sign outside this building says GIRLS WANTED. New York's garment industry included many such small sweatshops.

Life in a Sweatshop

What was it like working in a textile factory, sometimes called a sweatshop? We can get a glimpse of the harsh working conditions from Rose (Rahel) Gollup Cohen, who became a garment industry worker when she was still a girl. Rose was born on April 4, 1880, in western Russia, in what is today Belarus. Life was hard for Jewish people there. They were often victims of attacks and subject to harsh laws targeting Jewish families. Rose's father was able to escape and earn enough to send for Rose. In 1892, at age twelve, Rose joined him in the crowded tenements of New York City.

Rose wanted to work. She knew her job as a seamstress would help buy tickets so her mother and siblings could join them in America. Nevertheless, it was very hard. In a memoir, Rose wrote about her first day doing hand sewing in a sweatshop—and captured the power that bosses had over the workers, who had very few rights.

I lay awake long that night. I was eager to begin life on my own responsibility but was also afraid. We rose earlier than usual that morning for father had to take me to the shop and not be over late for his own work. I wrapped my thimble and scissors, with a piece of bread for breakfast, in a bit of newspaper, carefully stuck two needles into the lapel of my coat and we started.

In the shop, the boss put a coat down before her.

Her job was to finish the lining of the sleeves. Rose was paid by the piece rather than by the hour. She did well, but the boss was relentless, and never let her rest.

All day long I took my finished work and laid it on the boss's table. He would glance at the clock and give me other work. Before the day was over I knew that this was a "piece work shop," [and] that there were four machines and sixteen people were working. I also knew that I had done almost as much work as "the grown-up girls" and that they did not like me. . . .

Seven o'clock came and every one worked on. . . . My neck felt stiff and my back ached. I wished there were a back to my chair so that I could rest against it a little. When the people began to go home it seemed to me that it had been night a long time. . . . From this hour a hard life began for me.

Eyewitness to Tragedy

Horse-drawn fire wagons race to the Triangle Waist Company factory fire in New York City in 1911.

Like Ed Chamberlin in 1871 Chicago, a young reporter just happened to be on the scene on the Saturday afternoon of the Triangle fire. His name was William Shepherd.

"I was walking through Washington Square when a puff of smoke issuing from the factory building caught my eye. I reached the building before the alarm was turned in. I saw every feature of the tragedy visible from outside the building," William said.

William phoned in the story to his newspaper. To escape the smoke and fire, panicked workers went to the windows and dozens jumped to their deaths. William could have made it easy for his readers. He didn't. Even today, his story brings us into that awful moment.

"As I reached the scene of the fire, a cloud of smoke hung over the building . . . I looked up to the seventh floor. There was a living picture in each window—four screaming heads of girls waving their arms.

"'Call the firemen,' they screamed—scores of them. 'Get a ladder,' cried others. They were all as alive and whole and sound as were we who stood on the sidewalk. I couldn't help thinking of that. We cried to them not to jump. We heard the siren of a fire engine in the distance. The other sirens sounded from several directions.

"'Here they come,' we yelled. 'Don't jump; stay there.'"

But the firemen's ladders didn't reach high enough, nor were the safety nets strong enough to bear the weight of those who leaped. As William and others watched in helpless horror, some women and girls chose to jump rather than burn to death.

"The floods of water from the firemen's hose that ran into the gutter were actually stained red with blood," said William. "I remembered their great strike of last year in which these same girls had demanded more sanitary conditions and more safety precautions in the shops. These dead bodies were the answer."

Another eyewitness recalled hearing a hardened reporter on the scene remark, "I saw the *Slocum* disaster [the *General Slocum* steamship fire], but it was nothing to this."

The Triangle fire was a heartbreaking tragedy for those who lost loved ones that day. The event sent ripples of shock across the country. It spurred women in the labor union movement to keep struggling for better conditions.

Another eyewitness went on to change the lives of millions. Social worker Frances Perkins was having tea with a friend in Washington Square that afternoon and saw what happened. The next week, she attended a memorial gathering, where she heard labor activist Rose Schneiderman call for more support of a working-class movement.

In later speeches, Frances pointed to the Triangle factory fire as a turning point in her life. After the fire, she helped to investigate factory working conditions and pass new laws to improve factory safety. She went on to serve as secretary of labor in New York. The improvements in fire safety laws in that state became a model for better protections for workers throughout the country.

When New York governor Franklin D. Roosevelt won the presidency in 1932, he tapped Frances as secretary of labor, the first woman to be part of a presidential cabinet. In that important role, Frances continued her work on behalf of American workers and families. She championed unemployment insurance to help people when they lose their jobs and fought to limit child labor. Frances also spearheaded the effort to create the Social Security Act in 1935—a reform to protect people unable or too old to work, which continues to improve the lives of American families.

Historians can point to many fire safety improvements for workers made after the Triangle fire. But are workers always safe?

Unfortunately, no. In 1991, twenty-five of eighty-one workers died after a fire broke out at Imperial Food Products, a chicken processing plant in Hamlet, North Carolina. The sprinkler system failed, and again, doors were locked. Workers in many twenty-first-century workplaces still face obstacles to safe working conditions. The Triangle factory fire may have happened long ago, but it reminds us that the fight for justice, equality, and fair treatment for all continues.

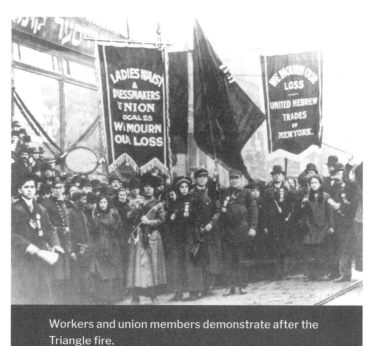

Workers and union members demonstrate after the Triangle fire.

A somber memorial parade for those killed at the Triangle factory took place in torrential rains.

Firefighters and the 9/11 Memorial Museum

The Triangle Waist Company fire was the deadliest workplace tragedy in the nation until another event, ninety years later, on September 11, 2001, when four coordinated attacks by Al-Qaeda terrorists claimed the lives of 2,777 Americans. Among other memorials, the 9/11 Memorial Museum on the site of the Twin Towers in New York City honors victims and first responders.

A total of 343 firefighters were killed on that day; more have since died from illnesses resulting from exposure to toxic substances during rescue and recovery efforts. In September 2020, FDNY, the Fire Department of New York, added 27 people, bringing this additional death toll to 227.

Begin your learning journey here: https://911tributemuseum.org/tribute-2-0/#Tribute-2.0:-Ready-To-Experience-The-9/11-Tribute-Museum.

Learn More about Fire Trucks & Firefighting History

Museums are a great place to start to explore antique fire engines and the history of firefighting. You can visit online or in person. Here are a few recommendations:

The **African American Firefighter Museum** in Los Angeles, California, is dedicated to preserving and sharing the history of African American firefighters. Visit it online at http://www.aaffmuseum.org/.

The Historical Society and Museum of the California Department of Forestry and Fire Protection has an online gallery of fire trucks dating back to 1929. https://calfirehistory.com/gallery/.

The **New York City Fire Museum** has online exhibits highlighting the history of firefighting, including a special 9/11 exhibit. Learn more at https://www.nycfiremuseum.org/on-display.

The Wrightsville School Fire, 1959

In 1940, Dr. Carter G. Woodson, founder of Black History Month, urged Americans to learn about all of our history. He wrote, "The teaching of the whole truth will help us in the direction of a real democracy."

Fires and natural disasters are often hard to read about. They hurt the poor, immigrants, and people of color the most. And as the Wrightsville School Fire shows, racism and racist policies cost lives.

The so-called "Negro Boys Industrial School" in Wrightsville, Arkansas, was a sort of work farm or reform school—but the awful conditions made it more like a brutal prison. Many boys were sent there for very small offenses or pranks. They endured cruel beatings, a lack of clean drinking water, not enough hot water for showers, and inadequate, horrible food. There was never enough money to run the school safely or properly. One report in 1956 noted that the boys had only rags for clothes and more than half didn't have socks in the winter.

In the early morning of March 5, 1959, a fire broke out at the school. The fire killed twenty-one innocent young people. Those who managed to escape had to claw their way through smoke and knock out two window screens. It was later found that sixty-nine boys had been padlocked into their dormitory.

The fire was largely covered up by the state's governor and other White officials who had no interest in exposing a long history of abuses against African Americans. Instead, they tried to put all the blame on the staff in charge of the school.

The University of Arkansas at Little Rock has a virtual exhibit about the fire. The exhibit notes, "The history of the Arkansas Negro Boys Industrial School, the fire which took the lives of 21 boys, and its shameful aftermath, were played out against a wider backdrop of an unyielding commitment to maintain white supremacy for as long as possible." No charges were ever filed against anyone in this case.

This fire is not as well known as it should be. At long last, on April 21, 2018, a memorial was placed in Haven of Rest Cemetery in Little Rock, Arkansas, where fourteen of the victims are buried. It took fifty years for this to happen. You can learn more about it at this University of Arkansas site: https://ualrexhibits.org/desegregation/tales-from -the-classroom/negro-boys-industrial-school-fire/.

CHAPTER TWELVE
Forests and Wildfire: A Look Back

We began this book with the 1871 wildfire in Peshtigo. In Part Two, we've explored fires in cities and buildings during the twentieth century. But we've skipped over one significant event: the deadly wildfires of 1910. That summer, wildfires broke out in several states, killing eighty-five people, mostly wildland firefighters.

The wildfires in 1910 had a huge impact on how America managed wildfires and forests for many years—issues we'll be talking about in the final part of this book. So, before we move on, let's take a look back.

We know the Peshtigo fire and others in the Midwest in 1871 caused a tremendous loss of life. These fires also destroyed many acres of forestland. The destruction of these forests worried people in the timber industry. After all, if the trees burned down, they couldn't be sold for profit. These losses supported the view that fire was a threat to growth and progress. This, of course, was in contrast to the ways many Native American communities lived with and actively managed forests and used fire to balance and cleanse the ecosystem.

The National Forest Foundation describes it this way: "Long before European settlers landed in North America, American Indians intentionally used fire to their advantage. Fire enabled them to alter and improve wildlife habitats, manage for agriculture, and clear travel routes . . . So, in addition to the natural fires that shaped the continent's forest landscapes, human-set fires further controlled forest fuels and perpetuated fire-adapted ecosystems.

"But as new settlers spread across the land—living within and depending upon the resources of the nation's forests—fire posed a threat to homes, livelihoods and lives. Wildfire was soon viewed as a beast to be tamed, like much of the wildness that was the West."

At the same time, as people saw this relentless development, some began to worry that there would be no forests and wild places left unless some were protected. A bill to create Yellowstone National Park, the first of now sixty-three national parks, was signed into law in 1872.

U.S. government efforts to preserve and manage forests date back to 1876. And in 1891, the U.S. Congress passed the Forest Reserve Act to authorize the president to designate some public lands as "forest reserves," later renamed "national forests." In 1905, the U.S. Forest Service was established. The agency took charge of managing national forests. Its first chief was a conservation leader named Gifford Pinchot. While the national effort to preserve forests did protect them from development, it also had a negative impact on Native American communities in many places. As just one example, in Northern California, some Native Americans who had been living within the boundaries of national forests lost their homes.

While the national parks fall under the Department

of the Interior, the U.S. Forest Service is part of the Department of Agriculture. For that reason, it's sometimes referred to as the USDA Forest Service. The agency manages 193 million acres of land. Most of our nation's public forests are owned by the federal government. The U.S. Forest Service works in partnership with states, tribes, local communities, and others to help steward other forestlands. The top priority of the U.S. Forest Service is to "maintain and improve the health, diversity, and productivity of the nation's forests and grasslands to meet the needs of current and future generations."

In 1898, shortly after the first forest reserves were established, the first professional school of forestry began as the New York State College of Forestry at Cornell University. The word **forestry** refers to the management of forests, primarily with the goal of harvesting timber. Increasingly, foresters also became involved in natural resources conservation, which includes protecting ecosystems and land for the benefit of wildlife, soil, water, and recreation.

The Fires of 1910 and the Big Blowup

The black dots on the map show the location of wildfires in the summer of 1910.

In 1910, when the U.S. Forest Service was only five years old, it faced a tremendous challenge. That summer, more than 1,700 wildfires broke out in Idaho, Washington, and Montana. The crisis culminated on August 20–21 with the Big Blowup (sometimes called the Big Burn). Driven by winds of hurricane force, fires spread rapidly. The fires of 1910 burned more than three million acres and killed at least eighty-five people.

In the most famous and terrifying incident during the Big Blowup, forest ranger Ed Pulaski and his team got trapped by a rapidly moving fire near Wallace, Idaho. Because he knew the area well, Ed was able to lead a group of firefighters to safety in a mine tunnel. His heroic actions saved the lives of forty-five men.

Aftermath: Fire Prevention and Suppression

The widespread fires and deaths of wildland firefighters made news across the country. Forest fire policies became part of the national conversation. The deadly fires of 1910 led to decades of national forest management policies that favored **fire suppression**, which means to prevent or put out fires as quickly as possible. These policies also affected tribal communities, who had been forcibly removed from their lands and not allowed to practice cultural burnings—the very practices that had been an integral part of the landscape for thousands of years.

Then, in 1935, the U.S. Forest Service adopted what became known as the "10 a.m. policy," which set a goal that all fires would be controlled by 10 a.m. the day after they were reported. This was also a kind of fire suppression. This policy ignored the natural role of fire in forest regeneration and fuel reduction and it called for more and more firefighters, who often had to work overnight in dangerous conditions to put fires out by an arbitrary time.

Many fires are started by human carelessness. To help educate people and prevent fires, the character Smokey Bear (often called Smokey the Bear) was introduced in 1944. In addition, more roads, fire tower lookouts, and ranger stations were built in national forests to help spot fires and make it easier for wildland firefighters to reach them.

These policies had a tremendous impact on forest management, not only in American forests but also in other countries that followed America's lead. Yet, as time went on, it became clear to government officials and the U.S. Forest Service what Native Americans and other Indigenous people all over the globe have known since the beginning of time: Strict fire suppression is not the answer to healthy forests.

A Legacy of Fire Suppression

In the 1970s, the Forest Service began to shift its policies on fighting wildfires. In 1971, the 10 a.m. policy was modified so that some wilderness fires were allowed to increase to ten acres if they didn't pose a danger to life or private property.

But changing fire suppression policies isn't easy. There are more homes and towns located closer to forests. It is natural that people worry about air quality, smoke, and safety. Timber industry workers and landowners may want fires to be suppressed because they think this protects their property from damage. These factors, along with decades of Forest Service fire suppression policies, have had a profound impact on the state of our forests today. In California, for example, aggressive fire suppression in the past has resulted in dense vegetation and left forests vulnerable to drought and bark beetles, killing more than 150 million trees in the state.

Forest expert Merv George, Jr., explains, "Our fuels problem in our country is not complicated. We have too much forest fuels (trees and brush). We got here by being good at putting all fires out for over a hundred years. We also got here by planting lots of trees that we have yet to harvest. How we deal with these fuels now . . . is where it gets complicated."

As we shall see in Part Three, dealing with that complicated picture is part of the challenges we face in the twenty-first century—a time when wildfires are reaching our very doorsteps.

Want to Be a Forester?

Meet Merv George, Jr., the U.S. Forest Service supervisor for the Rogue River-Siskiyou National Forest in Oregon and California. Merv grew up on the Hoopa Valley Indian Reservation, where he became the youngest tribal chairman at age twenty-four and spent fifteen years in tribal government. He received a degree in Native American Studies from Humboldt State University. Merv has said he sees his role as a bridge to foster relationships between Native communities and the Forest Service, as well as helping to educate the general public about using fire to sustain healthy forests. On the left is Merv's helicopter selfie!

There are many ways to enter a career in natural resources and forestry. It might start just by loving nature, taking walks, reading books, and noticing the trees, plants, birds, and insects near where you live.

Some people go to college to learn about this field and focus on specialties such as wildlife biology, climate change, forest ecology, or urban forestry (trees and plants in cities). There are even degree programs in wildland fire management that combine the science and operations, including the why and how of managing wildfires and controlled (prescribed) fires. Other programs such as the University of Arizona's Laboratory of Tree-Ring Research offers college classes and outreach programs that study the annual growth rings of trees.

Want to study right next to a forest? There are many options available, including the College of the Menominee Nation in Keshena, Wisconsin, which offers an associate's degree in Natural Resources and is open to students of all backgrounds.

Most of all, remember to notice and enjoy trees!

Billowing smoke and fierce, frequent fires are part of the new world of fire. Here, smoke rises from the Woolsey fire in November 2018 in Malibu, California.

Part Three

THE TWENTY-FIRST CENTURY
A New World of Fire

"Climate change has been a key factor in increasing the risk and extent of wildfires in the Western United States."

—CENTER FOR CLIMATE AND ENERGY SOLUTIONS

"It's taken us 100 years to get here ... It's going to take a long time to get our forests healthy again."

—MERV GEORGE, JR.

CHAPTER THIRTEEN
Facing Urgent Challenges

Wildfires that threaten residential communities have become more common in California. Here, the Canyon Fire 2 in 2017 threatens homes in Anaheim.

n August 2018, the U.S. Forest Service published a paper listing some of the challenges we face with wildfires today. The paper noted, "Managers and owners of forests across the Nation face urgent challenges, among them catastrophic wildfires, invasive species, drought, and epidemics of forest insects and disease.

"Of particular concern are longer fire seasons and the rising size and severity of wildfires, along with the expanding risk to communities, natural resources, and the safety of firefighters."

You probably already know something about **climate change** and **global warming**. Scientists have collected evidence that Earth's climate is getting warmer; summers are hotter; and there are more frequent droughts, which last longer. These changes are partly the result of burning fuels like coal and oil. When this happens, an invisible gas called carbon dioxide is released. These **carbon emissions** caused by burning fossil fuels like gas and oil get trapped in Earth's upper atmosphere, forming what some people call an invisible blanket that traps heat before it escapes to space. This is also called the greenhouse effect. And it's making our climate warmer and warmer.

It makes sense that wildfires are connected to climate change. We know there are more fires, they are more severe, and fire seasons in the western United States last longer. Years of drought have had an impact and have weakened trees, which are less able to fight off damaging insects, such as the bark beetle. When fires start, they are harder to control because the landscape has too much fuel due to past fire suppression policies. Plus, the warmer climate is more likely to dry out both dead and green fuels. Fires also burn longer at night, since nighttime temperatures don't cool off as much as they once did.

Wildfires also pose increasing risks to communities now since more people live in areas close to forests. These communities want and need electricity—and electricity requires transmission lines and equipment that must be maintained and can sometimes be the cause of sparks that start fires.

The U.S. Forest Service mentioned these challenges in the August 2018 report. And just three months later, in November of that year, a swift-moving, deadly fire broke out near the town of Paradise in northern

California. Called the Camp Fire, it became the deadliest wildfire since the summer of 1910.

Fire in Paradise

Just before 6:30 a.m. on the morning of Thursday, November 8, 2018, a worker for the utility company PG&E (Pacific Gas and Electric) spotted flames in a clearing underneath transmission wires in a canyon near Jarbo Gap in northern California.

Because of its location near a forest dirt track called Camp Creek Road, the fire was given the official name Camp Fire. It's also sometimes unofficially known as the Paradise Fire because of its devastating impact on one town.

As we saw in Peshtigo, drought and winds made the situation that day much worse. Back in 1871, railroad workers and sparks from railroads likely caused the blaze. In the Camp Fire and other California fires, faulty electrical equipment from PG&E was to blame. The Camp Fire is similar in another way to Peshtigo. You may remember that the fire in Peshtigo moved fast, like a freight train, driven by wind and lots of dry wood or available fuel. Back in 1871, the strong winds on the night of October 8 increased the amount of oxygen in the fire triangle, which sped up the rate of combustion, or burning, causing a fast-moving catastrophe.

In much the same way, on the morning of November 8, 2018, the Camp Fire also spread incredibly quickly—so quickly it wasn't possible to evacuate everyone in time. Paradise did have a sound evacuation plan, but no one expected *everyone* would have to leave at the same time.

The few roads leading out of town soon became clogged. Some residents, especially the elderly, were not able to leave in time, and almost all of the eighty-five people who died were age fifty or older. About 50,000 people evacuated; nearly 14,000 homes were destroyed. The Paradise fire was the most expensive disaster in 2018, not only in the United States but in the entire world. It caused $16.5 billion in losses.

After the tragedy, many Paradise residents decided to relocate to other places in California, as well as to other states, rather than return and rebuild. Students missed weeks of school and some completed the school year online or in temporary classrooms in nearby cities.

Burned out car from the Camp Fire in Paradise, California

In June 2020, the utility company PG&E pleaded guilty to causing the fire and deaths that resulted from it. PG&E agreed to pay $25.5 billion to victims and communities, and to take actions to reduce the future risk of wildfire.

The word *wildfire* makes us think of a fire that stays in the wild. But in our new world of fire, that's not necessarily so. Fires are now more frequent and severe, and come closer to residential communities, even major cities. Perhaps you already know what it's like to face the threat of wildfire. Perhaps your town has been

In November 2018, the Camp Fire destroyed most of the town of Paradise, California.

Fires in the West affect several states. This is an aerial view of homes and vehicles in a residential community destroyed by fire in 2020 in southern Oregon. During the 2020 wildfire season, 1.2 million acres in Oregon burned, nine people lost their lives, and more than 4,000 homes were destroyed.

covered in smoke from a nearby fire. Maybe you've had to evacuate your home; maybe your house, apartment building, or town has been in the path of flames.

Most experts believe destructive wildfire seasons in the West will only grow worse. No one wants deadly fires like that in Paradise to happen again. The fire management toolbox includes various ways of trying to prevent severe fires. For instance, electric companies in California and other wildfire-prone states are trying to reduce the risk by cutting electricity to customers during times of high winds and dry conditions. This helps prevent sparks from high-voltage wires from igniting fires. These programs, known as "public safety power shutoffs," are likely to become more common in the future.

Other changes will have to be made by our society as a whole, such as moving to electric cars instead of ones that use gas and heating our homes with different sources of energy, including wind and solar. People who live in areas prone to wildfires can also take actions to lower the risk of fire, such as designing residential communities and homes with fire risk in mind. This can include installing special fire-resistant roofs and siding, and using patios and driveways to create as much space as possible around the house. More people are learning about "firewise landscaping," which means choosing appropriate low-growing plants and a landscape design that helps protect a home from fire.

All these measures and more will be needed to help reduce the danger and damage wildfires can cause. At the same time, there is also a growing call for changes that go further—and transform how we think about and live in our new world of fire.

CHAPTER FOURTEEN
Our New World of Fire

Fires in the Amazon rain forest impact the world's climate.

When fire struck Peshtigo on October 8, 1871, it took a long time for news of the disaster to reach anyone on the outside. Today, though, our world is much more connected.

But that connection is more than just finding out about things that happen in other places. We now understand that events can ripple out and affect others far away, whether it's a new virus or a devastating fire in rain forests on another continent. Every day we are learning about and seeing more evidence of the many ways that humans, wildlife, oceans, and forests are all affected by climate change.

That's one reason the United States takes part in international efforts in public health, and why we partner with other nations to reduce carbon emissions caused by burning fossil fuels like oil and coal. It's why scientists from NASA (the National Aeronautics and Space Administration) study wildfires in the United States and around the globe. Climate change is leading to more long-lasting droughts and severe wildfires.

And it's also why people are coming together around the world to create new partnerships to help sustain healthy forests, do a better job in using fire to balance ecosystems, and also work to revitalize and restore landscapes and wildlife habitats after fires take place. The challenges are daunting. But they are also a chance to change, for the good of forests, people, wildlife, and our planet. The examples highlighted here are just a snapshot of some of the efforts underway.

Amazon Rain Forest

One area of special concern is the Amazon rain forest in Brazil. In November of 2019, NASA published a study showing that the atmosphere above the Amazon rain forest has been drying out, leaving this critical region more vulnerable to fires and drought.

"The Amazon is the largest rainforest on Earth. When healthy, it absorbs billions of tons of carbon dioxide (CO_2) a year through **photosynthesis**—the process plants use to convert CO_2, energy and water into food," notes the NASA study. "By removing CO_2 from the atmosphere, the Amazon helps to keep temperatures down and regulate climate. But it's a delicate system that's highly sensitive to drying and warming trends."

Scientists know that some fires in the rain forests are set intentionally to clear land for ranching and farming. Such deforestation takes a heavy toll on the forests and the Indigenous peoples who call the Amazon their home. Many people have been forced from their land. Reducing the intentional burning of forests is an urgent need. It will take change at many levels and will require nations and local communities to work together to find more equitable solutions.

Trees planted in the tropics are especially helpful in fighting global warming because they grow fast and capture more carbon. Recognizing this, in April 2021, an ambitious new public-private partnership called the LEAF (Lowering Emissions by Accelerating Forest finance) Coalition was announced at the 2021 Leaders Summit on Climate Change hosted by President Joe Biden.

The LEAF Coalition plans to mobilize $1 billion in financing to help protect tropical forests and those who depend on them, and support sustainable development. Find out more at https://leafcoalition.org/.

Creating solutions that work for local communities is key. In a 2020 *Washington Post* article, reporter Ben

Guarino featured the work of forest scientist Nestor Gregorio, a research fellow at Australia's University of the Sunshine Coast.

Gregorio and other forest researchers work with communities to help them find ways to care for forests and still make a living. For instance, instead of cutting down trees to plant crops, a community might grow fruit trees and native trees instead. At the same time, community members can manage other groves of trees for lumber in a sustainable way. This helps prevent deforestation and erosion, but still provides resources for families.

In his article, Guarino also captured some important insights foresters have about ways to help both communities and forests thrive: "'There is a saying in forestry: It is not about trees, it is about people,' said Nestor Gregorio. 'If people will find trees important, then they will look after the trees.'"

Bush Fires in Australia

In Australia, bush fires in the southern part of the country in 2019–2020 burned 46 million acres, killed at least thirty-four people, and had a devastating impact on wild creatures. Once again, exceptionally dry con-ditions as the result of a warming climate were major factors in this heartbreaking disaster.

Koala on Kangaroo Island. It's estimated that at least 30,000 koalas were killed during the devastating fires of 2019–2020 in Australia.

In the aftermath, some who want to help are now traveling to Australia through programs sometimes called "restorative tourism." This means people will

While thousands of kangaroos perished in bush fires, their overall survival is not as threatened as that of koalas and other species.

use vacation time to volunteer to help restore the land. Spending money as a tourist may help people whose jobs depend on visitors. But these sorts of programs enable visitors to contribute directly. For instance, volunteers might replant trees in areas devastated by fires, collect seeds, or help to monitor wildlife cameras.

In Australia's Northern Territory, the Kimberley Land Council, formed in 1978 by Kimberley Aboriginal people, who are the Indigenous inhabitants of Australia, is reinvigorating Indigenous fire management practices to protect the biodiversity of the Kimberley region.

"Highly skilled Indigenous rangers use traditional knowledge and techniques, together with modern science and technology, to fight fire with fire and reduce the likelihood of large uncontrolled wildfires," the council explains on its website.

Fires are set during the early dry season and burn slowly, creating a patchwork of burnt and unburnt land. Fuel that would have burned later in the dry season is removed to prevent severe fires and protect the habitat for wildlife and people.

America: Voices for Change and Restoration

Here in the United States, new partnerships are forming between tribes and U.S. government agencies to revitalize controlled burnings. Remember, these were once the furthest thing from how the U.S. Forest Service managed forests.

But, of course, it isn't new to foresters like Merv George, Jr. "It's not a foreign concept to those of us that come from the tribal communities," he says. "It's just what you do. It's why you're put on this earth—to take care of the landscapes that take care of you."

Now changes are taking place—changes that may help transform many people's ideas about fire. A National Public Radio (NPR) story in 2020 entitled "To Manage Wildfire, California Looks to What Tribes Have Known All Along," featured a two-day burning near Mariposa, in Northern California.

Led by Ron Goode, tribal chairman of the North Fork Mono, the event included members of tribal communities, state agency officials, townspeople, and university students. In her article, NPR reporter Lauren Sommer detailed the history of fire suppression and its impact on the landscape and on California tribal communities. (You can see photos of the burning and read the story by following the link in the Resources section.)

"Now, with wildfires raging across Northern California, joining other record-breaking fires from recent years, government officials say tackling the fire problem will mean bringing back 'good fire,' much like California's tribes once did," wrote Sommer.

This is already happening in some places. "In Northern California, the Karuk and Yurok tribes have partnered with the Forest Service to manage land for traditional values and wildfire management." Karuk is just one of a number of Native American communities in the United States at the forefront of climate change planning. In 2019, for example, the Karuk Tribe published its Climate Adaptation Plan. (See the Resources section for links.)

Another group bringing people together is the Fire Adapted Communities Learning Network (https://fireadaptednetwork.org/about/), a collaboration among a number of nonprofit and government partners. The Network is engaged in place-based efforts to change our relationships with fire and increase wildfire resilience. Its website reminds us that "connections change the world."

Connecting forests themselves is also part of an emerging vision for the future. Tribal leaders, environmentalists, and forest officials at the state and national levels are forging new partnerships. One is the concept of **anchor forests**. This model recognizes that sustainably managed forests, especially tribally owned, can help provide an anchor for cooperation and collaboration. Anchor forests can bring together different voices, landowners, and stakeholders with the common goal of healthy forests for the long term.

New leaders are emerging at the national level too. In March of 2021, Deb Haaland of New Mexico, an enrolled member of the Laguna Pueblo Tribe, became the first Native American secretary of the interior, overseeing national parks and the Department of Indian Affairs. When she was nominated in 2020, Secretary Haaland said:

A voice like mine has never been a Cabinet secretary or at the head of the Department of Interior. As our country faces the impacts of climate change and environmental injustice, the Interior has a role and I will be a partner in addressing these challenges by protecting our public lands and moving our country towards a clean energy future.

It's profound to think about the history of this country's policies to exterminate Native Americans and the resilience of our ancestors that gave me a place here today . . . I'm forever grateful and will do everything I can to be fierce for all of us, our planet, and all of our protected land. I am honored and ready to serve.

Sometimes, the challenges the world faces with wildfires and climate change seem too big for one person, family, school, community—or even country—to understand or tackle alone. But we are not alone.

You probably know of activist Greta Thunberg, who at fifteen started a one-person school strike for climate. She may have begun her campaign to fight climate change as a lone individual. But now her voice is joined by millions the world over.

The group Plant for the Planet grew out of the passion of nine-year-old Felix Finbeiner. Felix was inspired by Wangari Maathai, who won a Nobel Peace Prize for her effort to plant trees in Africa. Now children all over the globe are part of the effort.

However, you don't have to become a famous activist to begin to combat global warming, learn more about our new world of wildfire, or find out how to help keep forests healthy. You can make a start—by reading, taking a walk, listening to others, becoming involved in your community.

You might begin by noticing a tree. Or maybe you can plant one.

EXPLORE MORE
Activities and Resources

EXTRA! EXTRA! STUDENT REPORTER INTERVIEWS

Interested in being a reporter? You can start now. Some schools have their own television studios or newspapers. Scholastic Kids Press is a group of young reporters ages ten to fourteen who report the news. Their stories appear online and in issues of Scholastic *Classroom Magazines*, which reach more than 25 million students in classrooms nationwide. Check it out at https://kpcnotebook.scholastic.com/page/about-scholastic-kids-press. Need some examples? Here are two student interviews to spark your ideas.

Avery Griffis Interviews Former Wildland Firefighter Aili Johnston

Avery Griffis is a middle school student at the Lake Champlain Waldorf School in Shelburne, Vermont. He conducted an interview with Aili Johnston, who spent her college summers fighting wildfires. Following graduation, Aili provided training to wildland firefighters to improve working conditions for women and to help prevent discrimination against women working in the U.S. Forest Service.

Former wildland firefighter Aili Johnston loves mountain biking.

Aili Johnston (left) and her wildland firefighting sister, Meghan Johnston, pose in front of a fire truck.

Tell me a little bit about yourself!

I am 32 years old and love the outdoors. Mountain biking is my favorite, but skiing, hiking, rafting, and backpacking are all wonderful as well. It's so fun to be outside in the beauty of the world and spend time with my friends. It fills me up!

What made you want to be a firefighter?

My older sisters inspired me to become a wildland firefighter. They both did it before me and I always thought it sounded so cool and challenging. It was also the perfect summer job while I went to college.

What is your favorite thing about being a firefighter?

The people, that's the best and the worst part. You meet some really amazing people who become lifelong friends, and some silly folks that are fun to be around. But if you have a bad apple and they are always complaining, gossiping, or not participating, that can turn the crew cohesion inside out fast.

I also really liked to light the forest on fire! We weren't lighting the forest on fire willy-nilly. But sometimes you get put on a division responsible for creating a "burn line." That means you prepare a line (remove all flammables within thirty feet of a certain line). Then you light that line off so the main fire and the fire you started burn toward each other. This allows you to control, or contain, the main fire so it won't spread farther.

What do you do to get ready when called to a fire?

All the preparation comes way before you get the call. Along with staying in great physical condition, we have our "blue bags" packed— everything we need to be gone for twenty-one days such as clothing, a tent, and sleeping bag. When we get called, we have two hours to hit the road. I've fought fires in California, Washington, Oregon, Montana, Colorado, Wyoming, and I was even sent up to Alaska— the mosquitoes were TERRIBLE!

What was the worst fire that you fought and why?

Probably my first one, just because I had no idea what to expect. We held the line for twelve days straight. That means you stand on a line that's been burnt out and look into the unburnt forest and make sure there is no fire. Standing all day for twelve days was boring and my feet hurt. Firefighting is often a lot of boredom, sprinkled with such excitement.

How can we help prevent fires, as kids?

Be diligent about fire precautions in the summer. It's generally campfires that are lit in high fire danger that cause the worst fires and destroy the places many of us like to visit.

What advice would you give someone, boy or girl, who wants to fight fires as well?

If you want to do it—GO FOR IT! Make sure you train hard, otherwise you'll be hating yourself as you hike around the backwoods with your fifty-pound pack and a chain saw.
Be aware there is discrimination. Maybe it'll be different by the time you get a job, but women and people of color do have to prove themselves twice as hard as every White guy out there. Don't assume you know too much; you can learn a lot if you listen! Good luck.

To find out more about the history of women in wildland forest fighting, visit https://www.nationalforests.org/our-forests/your-national-forests-magazine/drawn-to-flame-women-forged-by-wildfire.

Lily Leibovitz and Hudson Leibovitz Interview Journalist Liel Leibovitz

Want to practice your interviewing skills? Why not start with a family member or adult you know? You might also interview your school librarian, custodian, or a neighbor. Like Bessie Bradwell of Chicago, Lily and Hudson Leibovitz live in a family where books are important. Their mom is an editor who helps make books for kids like this one, and Lily and Hudson aren't shy about giving their opinions. In this interview, they ask their dad, Liel Leibovitz, what it's like to be a writer and journalist.

What is it like to be a journalist? What does your job entail?

My job is to be curious: Whenever I have questions about anything or anyone, I ask them, and then write up what I learned. I talk to interesting people, visit interesting places, and then tell stories that help readers make sense of the world around them.

Why did you become a journalist?

Growing up, I was one of those kids who always asked questions: Why did you do that? Why did this just happen? What does it mean? So when I grew up, I wanted to have a job where I get to ask these questions and have people answer.

What is your favorite part of working as a journalist?

My favorite part about being a journalist is that no day is like the next. One day, you're hanging out with competitive eaters, shoving down hot dogs, and the next you're in Mongolia, riding horses in the Gobi Desert. Every day brings a new story and a new adventure.

What kind of training or classes did you have to take to become a journalist?

I did go to journalism school, but you really don't have to: If you'd like to become a journalist, take a pencil and a notebook, find something you'd like to learn more about, and then go out there and find out all about it. That's all there is to it.

What is the hardest or most challenging part of being a journalist?

When you're a journalist, people often want you to write nice things about them, and sometimes they tell you things that aren't exactly the truth, the whole truth, and nothing but the truth. The hardest part of the job is remaining respectful of the people you talk to while at the same time checking out what they tell you to make sure you aren't fooled.

What is the most important thing you've done as a journalist?

Speak up about issues that matter a great deal but don't get nearly enough attention, like the way we mistreat animals in factory farms.

What aspects of working as a journalist do you not like?

I don't like it when people lie to me, or flatter me, or try to manipulate me into writing something positive about them.

What kind of people do you interview?

I try to interview only people I admire and am deeply moved by, which, often, happens to be musicians, farmers, teachers, writers, and members of the clergy.

How do you find out about the stories you report on?

Fascinating stories are all around us! If you keep your eyes and your ears and your mind and your heart open, you'll never have a problem finding questions to ask and conversations to have and stories to write.

GLOSSARY

anchor forests Forests, often tribally managed, that serve as a model for bringing together many groups to cooperate and work together to create healthier and sustainable forests for the long-term.

carbon emissions The release of carbon into the atmosphere.

climate change A change in global or regional climate patterns. We use the term today to refer to increased levels of atmospheric carbon dioxide produced by the use of fossil fuels like oil or coal.

combustion A chemical reaction; its most common form is fire. Combustion produces heat and light. Most forms of combustion happen when oxygen joins with another substance. (When wood burns, oxygen in the air joins with the carbon in wood.) Combustion begins when a substance like wood or paper reaches a certain temperature, which is called its ignition point.

controlled (or prescribed) burns Intentional burnings often done in the cooler months of the year in order to clean the forest floor by removing forest "litter," such as weeds, small brush, and fallen branches, and to encourage the growth of new plants and to allow wildlife to thrive.

earthquake A shaking of the ground caused by movements within Earth's crust.

epicenter The point on Earth's surface above the focus of an earthquake.

fault In geology, a fault is a fracture or zones of fracture between two blocks of rock. Faults in Earth's crust allow the blocks to move against each other.

fire suppression The policy of putting out and stopping all forest wildfires from burning.

fire triangle The three elements needed for something to ignite: heat, fuel, and an oxidizing agent such as air.

foreshock A mild tremor that comes before the violent shaking of an earthquake.

forestry The management of forested land, primarily for harvesting timber but also to conserve and protect the forest.

global warming The gradual increase in the overall temperature of Earth's atmosphere caused by higher levels of heat-trapping gases like carbon dioxide and methane.

Great Midwest Fires of 1871 Term used to describe the fires of October 1871 in the Midwest, which burned over a million acres in several states and included the Peshtigo fire and the Great Chicago Fire.

hypothermia A dangerously low body temperature, usually caused by exposure to cold.

meteorologist A scientist who studies weather.

photosynthesis The process by which green plants and trees use sunlight to make their food.

primary source The term historians use to describe

a letter, document, piece of art, object, or recording created at the time of an event.

Richter scale Named for Charles Richter, who developed it in 1935, this numerical scale measures the strength of earthquakes. The scale begins at 1 and goes to 9 and higher. The Great Chilean Earthquake of 1960, placed at 9.4–9.6 on the scale, is the most powerful ever recorded.

San Andreas fault This fault extends vertically in California and is the boundary between the North American plate and the Pacific plate. Plates, also called tectonic plates, are slabs of rock, and are part of Earth's outer shell.

slash Debris such as small tree limbs and branches left by logging operations.

sustainable forestry A practice of managing forests that tries to balance conserving forests with using trees for the needs of people.

TEST YOUR KNOWLEDGE
Fill in the Blanks

Global _____ change is one factor leading to longer and more intense wildfires.

The deadliest fire in American history took place in the village of _____, Wisconsin.

One important tool for fire safety is to make sure your home has working _____ alarms.

The first rule for fire safety when leaving a building is _____ out and stay out.

After spending hours in a river to avoid fire, Father Peter Pernin and other survivors were at risk of _____.

The 1906 San Francisco fire broke out shortly after an _____ that occurred early on the morning of April 18.

Today's wildland firefighters work closely with _____, scientists who study weather.

Fire experts are recognizing the importance of using more prescribed or _____ burns to maintain healthy forests and prevent larger, more severe fires.

Heat, an oxidizing agent, and fuel are the three elements of the _____.

ANSWERS:
CLIMATE
PESHTIGO
SMOKE
GET
HYPOTHERMIA
EARTHQUAKE
METEOROLOGISTS
CONTROLLED
FIRE TRIANGLE

› **191** ‹

INTERNET RESOURCES

Please note that websites can change. If you need assistance, ask a librarian!

Fire Safety

American Red Cross Emergency Preparedness. https://www.redcross.org/get-help/how-to-prepare-for-emergencies/teaching-kids-about-emergency-preparedness/prep-champion.html.

NFPA (National Fire Protection Association) Learn Not to Burn program. https://www.nfpa.org/Public-Education/Teaching-tools/Learn-not-to-burn.

Smokey Bear. https://smokeybear.com/en/smokey-for-kids.

Sparky the Fire Dog. http://www.sparky.org/.

Nineteenth-Century Fires

The Great Fire of Chicago. PBS American Experience. https://www.pbs.org/wgbh/americanexperience /features/chicago-fire/.

The Great Chicago Fire & the Web of Memory. https://www.greatchicagofire.org/great-chicago-fire/.

Peshtigo Fire Museum.

http://www.peshtigofiremuseum.com/.

Twentieth-Century Fires

The *General Slocum*. https://www.nypl.org/blog /2011/06/13/great-slocum-disaster-june-15-1904.

Iroquois Theater. http://www.iroquoistheater.com /newspaper-coverage-iroquois-theater-fire-disaster .php.

Iroquois Theater and Fire Safety. https://www .smithsonianmag.com/history/how-theater-blaze -killed-hundreds-forever-changed-way-we-approach -fire-safety-180969315/.

San Francisco Fire—Interview of Lily Sung, Chinese Historical Society of America. https://www .chsa.org/wp-content/uploads/2013/04/Lily-Sung.pdf.

Triangle Fire. Kheel Center. https://trianglefire.ilr
.cornell.edu/.

Wildfires of 1910. Edward C. Pulaski of the U.S.
Forest Service. https://www.fs.usda.gov/detail/r1/learning
/history-culture/?cid=stelprdb5122876.

Wildfires of 1910. Forest History Society. https://
foresthistory.org/research-explore/us-forest-service
-history/policy-and-law/fire-u-s-forest-service
/famous-fires/the-1910-fires/.

Twenty-First-Century Fires and Climate Change

Climate Change—NOAA (National Oceanic and
Atmospheric Administration). https://www.noaa.gov
/education/resource-collections/climate/climate-change
-impacts.

Fire Adapted Communities Learning Network.
https://fireadaptednetwork.org/.

Indigenous Fire Management of the Kimberley
Land Council in Australia. https://www.klc.org.au
/indigenous-fire-management.

International Association of Wildland Fire: Learn

more about the global wildland fire community. https://www.iawfonline.org/

Karuk Tribe. https://www.karuk.us/index.php /departments/natural-resources/525-climate-adaptation.

LEAF Coalition. https://www.leafcoalition.org.

Native American Sustainable Forest Practices. https://qz.com/1904925/the-untapped-value-of -native-american-fire-management-techniques/.

NPR Environment. Sommer, Lauren. "To Manage Wildfire, California Looks to What Tribes Have Known All Along." https://www.npr.org/2020/08/24/899422710 /to-manage-wildfire-california-looks-to-what-tribes-have -known-all-along.

Paradise (aka Camp) Fire. Mooallem, Jon. "We Have Fire Everywhere." *New York Times Magazine.* https://www.nytimes.com/interactive/2019/07/31 /magazine/paradise-camp-fire-california.html.

Plant for the Planet. https://www1.plant-for-the -planet.org/.

Wildfires—NOAA (National Oceanic and Atmospheric Administration). https://www.noaa.gov /topic-tags/wildfires.

Women in Wildland Fire Fighting. Wallian, Dayle. "Drawn to Flame: Women Forged by Fire." *Your National Forests Magazine.* National Forest Foundation, Summer/Fall 2017. https://www.nationalforests.org/our-forests/your-national-forests-magazine/drawn-to-flame-women-forged-by-wildfire.

Yale Environment 360. Jones, Nicola. "How Native Tribes Are Taking the Lead on Planning for Climate Change." https://e360.yale.edu/features/how-native-tribes-are-taking-the-lead-on-planning-for-climate-change.

SUGGESTIONS FOR FURTHER READING

Auch, M. J. *Ashes of Roses*. New York: Square Fish, 2015.

Hoobler, Dorothy and Thomas. *What Was the San Francisco Earthquake?* New York: Penguin Workshop, 2016.

Hopkinson, Deborah. *Into the Firestorm: A Novel of San Francisco, 1906*. New York: Knopf, 2006.

————. *Shutting Out the Sky: Life in the Tenements of New York, 1880–1924*. New York: Scholastic, 2003.

Lee, Milly. Illustrated by Yangsook Choi. *Earthquake*. New York: Farrar, Straus and Giroux, 2006.

Murphy, Jim. *The Great Fire*. New York: Scholastic, 1995.

Philbrick, Raymond. *Wildfire: A Novel*. New York: Scholastic, 2021.

Tarshis, Lauren. *I Survived the Great Chicago Fire, 1871*. New York: Scholastic, 2015.

————. *I Survived the California Wildfires, 2018.* New York: Scholastic, 2020.

Wolff, Ashley. *Wildfire!* New York: Beach Lane Books, 2021.

SELECTED BIBLIOGRAPHY

(Note: Source Notes include additional sources and websites consulted.)

Cohen, Rose. Introduction by Thomas Dublin. *Out of the Shadow: A Russian Jewish Girlhood on the Lower East Side*. Ithaca: Cornell University Press, 1995.

Colbert, Elias, and Everett Chamberlin. *Chicago and the Great Conflagration*. Chicago: First Rate Publishers, 2020. (print on demand) Reprint.

Davies, Andrea Rees. *Saving San Francisco: Relief and Recovery after the 1906 Disaster*. Philadelphia: Temple University Press, 2012.

Ferguson, Gary. *Land on Fire: The New Reality of Wildfire in the West*. Portland, OR: Timber Press, 2017.

Gee, Alastair, and Dani Anguiano. *Fire in Paradise: An American Tragedy.* New York: W. W. Norton, 2020.

Gess, Denise, and William Lutz. *Firestorm at Peshtigo: A Town, Its People, and the Deadliest Fire in American History.* New York: Henry Holt, 2002.

Lowe, David. *The Great Chicago Fire in Eyewitness Accounts and 70 Contemporary Photographs and Illustrations.* New York: Dover, 1979.

McIlvaine, Mabel. *Reminiscences of Chicago During the Great Fire.* Chicago: University of Michigan Library, reprints from the collection of the University of Michigan Library, 2020.

O'Donnell, Edward T. *Ship Ablaze: The Tragedy of the Steamboat* General Slocum. New York: Broadway Books, 2003.

Pernin, Peter. *The Great Peshtigo Fire: An Eyewitness Account.* Madison: State Historical Society of Wisconsin, 1999.

Pyne, Stephen J. *Fire: A Brief History.* Seattle: University of Washington Press, 2001.

———. *Year of the Fires: The Story of the Great Fires of 1910.* New York: Viking, 2010.

Smith, Carl. *Chicago's Great Fire: The Destruction and Resurrection of an Iconic American City.* New York: Atlantic Monthly Press, 2020.

Smith, Dennis. *San Francisco Is Burning: The Untold Story of the 1906 Earthquake and Fire.* New York: Plume, 2006.

Struzik, Edward. *Firestorm: How Wildfire Will Shape Our Future.* Washington, DC: Island Press, 2017.

Von Drehle, David. *Triangle: The Fire That Changed America.* New York: Atlantic Monthly Press, 2003.

SOURCE NOTES

Source notes are like the evidence a detective collects to make a case. They tell us where an author got a fact or a quotation. A note to teachers, educators, and adult readers: You may find references to scholarly articles in the notes that have not been included in the bibliography because of space considerations.

Prologue

"gleaming everywhere with fires.": Pernin, *The Great Peshtigo Fire: An Eyewitness Account*, 16.
"We went on and on . . .": Ibid.
"the crackling of a tiny tongue . . .": Ibid., 17.

Chapter One

"Good fires are ones . . .": Merv George, Jr. Facebook post, 6/4/2019. Used with permission.
"My horse held back . . .": Pernin, 18.
"distant roaring . . .": Ibid., 26.
"a traditional quality of life . . .": Menominee Tribal Enterprises. https://www.mtewood.com/SustainableForestry.

Source Notes

Chapter Two

"The air was no longer . . .": Pernin, 30–31.
"The roar increased . . .": Frank Tilton. *"Sketch of the Great Fires in Wisconsin." Green Bay Historical Bulletin*, Vol. 7, Nos. 1-2 (Jan-Jun 1931), 31.
"Within half an hour . . .": Pernin, 32.

Chapter Three

"The flames darted over . . .": Pernin, 31.
"'Father, beware, you are . . .'": Ibid., 35.
"I could scarcely . . .": Ibid., 37.

Chapter Four

"I could not unclose . . .": Pernin, 38.
"'When I heard the roar . . .'": Tilton, 36.
"Some of the young men . . .": Pernin, 39.
"Of the houses, trees . . .": Ibid., 43.
"'Father, do you know . . .'": Ibid., 49.

More on The Great Midwest Fires of 1871

Cause of the fires: "The Great Midwest Wildfires of 1871." National Weather Service. https://www.weather.gov/grb/peshtigofire2.

Chapter Five

Chicago fire statistics: Pernin, xi.
Chicago population: C. Smith, *Chicago's Great Fire*, 16, 283.
Chicago industries: Ibid., 12–13.
"I was at the scene . . .": Quoted in McIlvaine, *Reminiscences of Chicago during the Great Fire*, 1.
"I stepped in . . .": Ibid., 2.

Chicago fire department; fires: C. Smith, 23–25. Also see PBS American Experience: Chicago on Fire: https://www.pbs.org/wgbh/americanexperience/features/chicago-fire/.

"Streams [of water] were thrown . . .": Quoted in McIlvaine, 2.

"All these things . . .": Ibid., 7.

"Though mostly of brick . . .": Ibid., 3.

"The wind had increased . . .": Ibid., 5.

"When I came down . . .": Quoted in McIlvaine, 15.

"I kept on . . .": Ibid., 16.

"I don't think . . .": Ibid.

"but the walks were . . .": Ibid., 17.

"Wherever I could see . . .": Ibid., 20.

"The roadway was full . . .": Ibid., 21.

"The Court-house . . .": Ibid., 33–35.

Chapter Six

"'This is a good thing . . .'": Bessie Bradwell, "The Great Chicago Fire & the Web of Memory." https://www.greatchicagofire.org/anthology-of-fire-narratives/bessie-bradwell/.

"storm of falling fire . . .": Quoted in McIlvaine, 25.

"It was like a snowstorm . . .": Bradwell.

"By chance, I met . . .": Ibid.

"People would run up to me . . .": Ibid.

"His first words were . . .": Ibid.

"'Don't worry . . .'": Ibid.

"Monday morning at three o'clock . . .": Fannie Belle Becker, "The Great Chicago Fire & the Web of Memory." https://www.greatchicagofire.org/anthology-of-fire-narratives/fannie-belle-becker/.

Chapter Seven

"Then a curious-looking . . .": Quoted in McIlvaine, 12.

"They saw the fire . . .": Ibid., 13.

Destruction: C. Smith, 93.

"forever exonerate Mrs. O'Leary . . .": Ibid., 305.

Chapter Eight

"We were told . . .": Quoted in McIlvaine, 305.

"We drew big crowds": Eddie Foy. "A Tragedy Remembered." *NFPA Journal* (National Fire Protection Association), July/August 1995, 75–79. https://www.nfpa.org/-/media/Files/Public-Education/By-topic /Occupancies/iroquois.ashx.

"It struck me . . ."; "stow him . . .": Ibid., 76.

"I jerked my door open . . .": Ibid.

"Probably not 40 seconds . . .": Ibid., 76–77.

"'Take my boy . . .'": Ibid., 77.

"'Take your time, folks . . .'": Ibid., 77–78.

"Then came a cyclonic blast . . .": Ibid., 78.

"But by this time . . .": Ibid., 78.

"As I rushed out . . .": Ibid., 79.

Chicago fire safety violations: C. Smith, 112–13.

Chapter Nine

"Wednesday morning, April 18 . . .": Elsie Cross. "Elsie H. Cross letters to Ruth, Oakland, California, May 17–28, 1906." MS 3469; California Historical Society, https://californiahistoricalsociety.org /blog/childrens-voices-from-the-archives-remembering-the-1906 -earthquake-and-fire/.

Forty-two engines: Davies. *Saving San Francisco*, 17.

"The low water supply . . .": Ibid., 18.

"Within an hour . . .": Jack London. "Story of an Eyewitness." California Parks and Recreation, https://www.parks.ca.gov/?page_id=24206. London's account originally appeared in *Collier's* magazine, May 6, 1906.

"Wednesday afternoon . . .": Cross.

"as bright as day . . .": Ibid.

"The next day in the morning . . .": Ibid.

Measuring Earthquakes

San Francisco earthquake: USGS. "The Great 1906 San Francisco

Earthquake." https://earthquake.usgs.gov/earthquakes/events/1906 calif/18april/.

San Andreas fault study: Structural Engineers Association of Northern California. https://legacy.seaonc.org/event/sfearthquake/.

Chapter Ten

Chinatown population: Davies, 25.

"As the few . . .": Ibid., 26.

"San Francisco's earthquake . . .": Ibid., 142.

"The week before . . .": Connie Young Yu, "Interview of Lily Sun on Her 1906 Earthquake Experience," interviewed in 1980. Chinese Historical Society. https://www.chsa.org/wp-content/uploads/2013/04 /Lily-Sung.pdf., 2.

"there were crowds . . .": Ibid.

"So sister said . . .": Ibid., 3.

"Here was the water . . .": Ibid.

"At nighttime we had . . .": Ibid.

"And, oh my . . .": Ibid.

"And they finally found us . . .": Ibid.

John the Rat-Catcher

"There was a bubonic plague scare . . .": John J. Conlon. April 18, 1906. Museum of the City of San Francisco. http://www.sfmuseum.net /1906/ew10.html.

Chapter Eleven

"We went from machine to machine . . .": Anna Pidone. Kheel Center of Cornell University. Leon Stein Survivor Interview. https://trianglefire .ilr.cornell.edu/primary/survivorInterviews/AnnaPidone.html.

Life in a Sweatshop

"I lay awake . . .": Cohen. *Out of the Shadow: A Russian Jewish Girlhood on the Lower East Side,* 108.

"All day long . . .": Ibid., 110–11.

"I was walking through . . .": William Shepherd. Kheel Center of Cornell University. Testimonials. https://trianglefire.ilr.cornell.edu/primary /testimonials/ootss_WilliamShepherd.html.

"As I reached . . .": Ibid.

"The floods of water . . .": Ibid.

"'I saw the *Slocum* . . .'": Charles Willis Thompson. Letter to Wm, April 14, 1911. https://trianglefire.ilr.cornell.edu/primary/letters/Charles WillisThompson.html.

Imperial fire: https://www.smithsonianmag.com/history/deadly-1991-hamlet -fire-exposed-high-cost-cheap-180964816/.

The Wrightsville School Fire

"The teaching of the whole truth . . .": Carter G. Woodson. *Negro History Bulletin*, Vol 4, No. 3, December 1940, 72.

1956 report: "Negro Boys Industrial School Fire of 1959." *Encyclopedia of Arkansas*. https://encyclopediaofarkansas.net/entries/negro -boys-industrial-school-fire-of-1959-5500/.

Arkansas school tragedy: Ibid.

"The history of the Arkansas . . .": Grif Stockley. "Negro Boys Industrial School Fire." https://ualrexhibits.org/desegregation/tales-from-the -classroom/negro-boys-industrial-school-fire/.

Chapter Twelve

"Long before European settlers . . .": National Forest Foundation, "Blazing Battles: The 1910 Fire and Its Legacy." https://www.nationalforests.org/our-forests/your-national-forests -magazine/blazing-battles-the-1910-fire-and-its-legacy.

History of U.S. Forest Service: "U.S. Forest Service Fire Suppression." Forest History Society. https://foresthistory.org/research-explore /us-forest-service-history/policy-and-law/fire-u-s-forest-service/u-s -forest-service-fire-suppression/

"maintain and improve . . .": U.S. Forest Service. https://www.fs.usda.gov /managing-land/national-forests-grasslands.

"10 a.m." policy: Gerald W. Williams. *The USDA Forest Service: The First*

Century. https://www.fs.usda.gov/sites/default/files/media/2015/06 /The_USDA_Forest_Service_TheFirstCentury.pdf, 33.

Impact of 1910 on national fire policy: "The 1910 Fires." Forest History Society. https://foresthistory.org/research-explore/us-forest-service-history/policy-and-law/fire-u-s-forest-service/famous-fires/ the-1910-fires/.

Ten-acre policy: Williams, 33.

California vegetation: Sophie Quinton and Alex Brown. "California May Need More Fire to Fix Its Wildfire Problem." *Stateline*, September 18, 2020. Pew Charitable Trust. https://www.pewtrusts .org/en/research-and-analysis/blogs/stateline/2020/09/18 /california-may-need-more-fire-to-fix-its-wildfire-problem

"Our fuels problem . . .": Merv George, Jr. Facebook post, 6/4/2019. Used with permission of the author.

Part Three

"Climate change has been . . .": "Wildfires and Climate Change." Center for Climate and Energy Solutions. https://www.c2es.org/content /wildfires-and-climate-change/.

"'It's taken us . . .'": Quoted in Shannon Gormley. "Oregon's Indigenous Communities Know How to Stop Megafires. Will the State Let Them?" *Willamette Week*, October 7, 2020. https://www.wweek .com/news/2020/10/07/oregons-indigenous-communities-know -how-to-stop-megafires-will-the-state-let-them/.

Chapter Thirteen

"Managers and owners . . .": U.S. Department of Agriculture. "Toward Shared Stewardship Across Landscapes," August 2018. https://www .fs.usda.gov/sites/default/files/toward-shared-stewardship.pdf.

14,000 homes: Gee and Anguiano. *Fire in Paradise*, 188–89.

Cost: Ibid., 202.

PG&E guilty plea: PG&E. "PG&E Statement on Company's Guilty Plea Related to 2018 Camp Fire," June 16, 2020. https://www.pge.com /en/about/newsroom/newsdetails/index.page?title=20200616_pge _statement_on_companys_guilty_plea_related_to_2018_camp_fire.

Source Notes

Oregon wildfire statistics: Governor Kate Brown. "State of the State Address," January 21, 2021. https://drive.google.com/file/d/1Ng5nd Pup99JALP5QWZQHrYp7M1z-Dejo/view.

Chapter Fourteen

"The Amazon is the largest rainforest . . .": NASA. "Human Activities Are Drying Out the Amazon," November 5, 2019. https://climate.nasa.gov/news/2928/human-activities-are-drying-out-the -amazon-nasa-study/.

"'There is a saying . . .'": Ben Guarino. "The Audacious Effort to Reforest the Planet." *Washington Post*, January 22, 2020. https://www.washingtonpost.com/graphics/2020/climate-solutions /trillion-tree-reforestation-climate-change-philippines/.

Koalas: Todd Woody. "Koalas and other marsupials struggle to recover from Australia's bushfires." *National Geographic,* July 17, 2020. https://www.nationalgeographic.com/animals/article/australia -marsupials-struggling-after-fires.

"Highly skilled . . .": Indigenous Fire Management, Kimberley Land Council. https://www.klc.org.au/indigenous-fire-management.

"'It's not a foreign concept . . .'": Quoted in Gormley.

"Now, with wildfires . . .": Lauren Sommer. "To Manage Wildfire, California Looks To What Tribes Have Known All Along." NPR Environment, August 24, 2020. https://www.npr.org/2020/08/24/899422710/to -manage-wildfire-california-looks-to-what-tribes-have-known-all-along.

"connections change the world . . .": Fire Adapted Communities Learning Network. https://fireadaptednetwork.org/.

"A voice like mine . . .": Official statement of Deb Haaland, on historic nomination to Interior secretary. *The Hill*, December 17, 2020. https://thehill.com/policy/energy-environment/530771-read-deb -haalands-official-statement-on-historic-nomination-to.

PHOTOGRAPH AND ILLUSTRATION CREDITS

Photos ©: 10–11: Wisconsin Historical Society; 12: Library of Congress; 24: Bettmann/Getty Images; 28: The Granger Collection; 30: Forest History Society, Durham, N.C.; 34, 43, 44: Wisconsin Historical Society; 47, 50, 55: Chicago History Museum; 56, 61: Library of Congress; 62: Chicago History Museum; 64, 73, 74: Library of Congress; 76: Chicago History Museum; 78–79: Library of Congress; 80–81: National Archives; 91: Chicago History Museum; 92–93: Library of Congress; 99 left: FLHC A110/Alamy Stock Photo; 99 right: The New York Public Library, Astor, Lenox and Tilden Foundation; 100: Library of Congress; 103, 104: National Archives; 107: Library of Congress; 109, 118: National Archives; 121, 122, 123 top and bottom, 126, 129, 132: Library of Congress; 136: National Archives; 137: Library of Congress; 147: Forest History Society, Durham, N.C.; 152 left: Merv George, Jr.; 152 right: Courtesy of the *Willamette Week*; 179: Aili Johnston; 180: Victoria E. Hemphill. All other photos © Shutterstock.com.

INDEX

ACKNOWLEDGMENTS

Thank you for reading *The Deadliest Fires Then and Now*, the third book in the Deadliest series. I began writing at home in Oregon during the devastating wildfire season of 2020. As I finish this book, in summer 2021, once again the western United States is experiencing severe drought and wildfires, made worse by the effects of human-caused climate change. I hope reading this book will inspire readers, young and old, to take action to help restore the Earth and protect people, forests, and wildlife.

This book would not have been possible without the brilliant vision of editor Lisa Sandell. I'm also grateful to my agent, Steven Malk, and to the dedicated team at Scholastic, including Ellie Berger, David Levithan, Lizette Serrano, Emily Heddleson, Jordana Kulak, Lauren Donovan, Erin Berger, Rachel Feld, Laura Beets, Kelli Boyer, Jalen Garcia-Hall, Keirsten Geise, Becky Terhune, Elizabeth Krych, Lisa Broderick, Jael

Fogle, Cian O'Day, Emily Teresa, John Pels, Lori Benton, and the fabulous Scholastic sales force.

Any errors or mistakes in this book are mine. There would be many more without the contributions of several individuals who brought their expertise, knowledge, and diverse perspectives to the project. Special thanks to Merv George, Jr., Ron Steffens, and Francis Vigil. This book is immensely better thanks to their assistance.

I also wish to thank educators, teachers, librarians, and parents for encouraging young people to read nonfiction—and to write. I'm especially grateful to Avery Griffis and Aili Johnston for their piece on wildland firefighting; to Avery's teacher, Rebekah Hopkinson of Lake Champlain Waldorf School for helping make the interview with Aili possible; and to the entire Hemphill-Johnston family. Thanks also to the sister-and-brother interview team of Lily and Hudson Leibovitz for their interview of their dad, journalist Liel Leibovitz. I hope the Deadliest series inspires other young writers too.

Finally, as always, I am grateful from the bottom of my heart to my friends and family. Andy, Dimitri, Rebekah, Eric, and Oliver—I love you more than words can say.

ABOUT THE AUTHOR

Deborah Hopkinson is an award-winning author of picture books, middle grade fiction, and nonfiction. Her nonfiction titles include *We Must Not Forget: Holocaust Stories of Survival and Resistance; We Had to Be Brave: Escaping the Nazis on the Kindertransport*, a Sydney Taylor Notable Book and finalist for the Oregon Book Award; *Titanic: Voices from the Disaster*, a Sibert Medal Honor Book and YALSA Award for Excellence in Nonfiction finalist; *Courage & Defiance: Stories of Spies, Saboteurs, and Survivors in World War II Denmark*, a Sydney Taylor Notable Book, NCTE Orbis Pictus Recommended Book, and a winner of the Oregon Book Award and Oregon Spirit Award; *Dive! World War II Stories of Sailors & Submarines in the Pacific*, an NCTE Orbis Pictus Recommended Book and Oregon Spirit Award Honor Book; and *D-Day: The World War II Invasion That Changed History*; as well as *The Deadliest Hurricanes Then and Now* and *The Deadliest Diseases Then and Now.*

Deborah lives with her family near Portland, Oregon. Visit her online at www.deborahhopkinson.com and follow her on Twitter at @Deborahopkinson and on Instagram at @deborah_hopkinson.